The Cloud of Unknowing

The Classic of Medieval Mysticism

Edited by

Evelyn Underhill

DOVER PUBLICATIONS, INC.
Mineola, New York

Bibliographical Note

This Dover edition, first published in 2003, is an unabridged republication of the work originally published by Stuart & Watkins, London, in 1912.

Library of Congress Cataloging-in-Publication Data

The cloud of unknowing : the classic of medieval mysticism / edited by Evelyn Underhill.
    p. cm.
  Originally published: 1st ed. London : Stuart & Watkins, 1912.
  ISBN 0-486-43203-3 (pbk.)
  1. Mysticism—History—Middle Ages, 600–1500. I. Underhill, Evelyn, 1875–1941.

BV5080.C54 2003
248.22—dc21

                                                    2003048962

Manufactured in the United States of America
Dover Publications, Inc., 31 East 2nd Street, Mineola, N.Y. 11501

Introduction

THE LITTLE FAMILY of mystical treatises which is known to students as "the Cloud of Unknowing group," deserves more attention than it has hitherto received from English lovers of mysticism: for it represents the first expression in our own tongue of that great mystic tradition of the Christian Neoplatonists which gathered up, remade, and "salted with Christ's salt" all that was best in the spiritual wisdom of the ancient world.

That wisdom made its definite entrance into the Catholic fold about A.D. 500, in the writings of the profound and nameless mystic who chose to call himself "Dionysius the Areopagite." Three hundred and fifty years later, those writings were translated into Latin by John Scotus Erigena, a scholar at the court of Charlemagne, and so became available to the ecclesiastical world of the West. Another five hundred years elapsed, during which their influence was felt, and felt strongly, by the mystics of every European country: by St. Bernard, the Victorines, St. Bonaventura, St. Thomas Aquinas. Every reader of Dante knows the part which they play in the *Paradiso*. Then, about the middle of the 14th century, England—at that time in the height of her great mystical period—led the way with the first translation into the vernacular of the Areopagite's work. In *Dionise Hid Divinite*, a version of the *Mystica Theologia*, this spiritual treasure-house was first made accessible to those outside the professionally religious class. Surely this is a fact which all lovers of mysticism, all "spiritual patriots," should be concerned to hold in remembrance.

It is supposed by most scholars that *Dionise Hid Divinite*, which—appearing as it did in an epoch of great spiritual vitality—quickly attained to a considerable circulation, is by the same hand which wrote the *Cloud of Unknowing* and its companion books; and that this hand also produced an English paraphrase of Richard of St. Victor's *Benjamin Minor*, another work of much authority on the contemplative life. Certainly the influence of Richard is only second to that of Dionysius in this unknown mystic's own work—work, however, which owes as much to the deep personal experience and extraordinary psychological gifts of its writer, as to the tradition that he inherited from the past.

Nothing is known of him; beyond the fact, which seems clear from his writings, that he was a cloistered monk devoted to the contemplative life. It has been thought that he was a Carthusian. But the rule of that austere order, whose members live in hermit-like seclusion, and scarcely meet except for the purpose of divine worship, can hardly have afforded him opportunity of observing and enduring all those tiresome tricks and absurd mannerisms of which he gives so amusing and realistic a description in the lighter passages of the *Cloud*. These passages betray the half-humorous exasperation of the temperamental recluse, nervous, fastidious, and hypersensitive, loving silence and peace, but compelled to a daily and hourly companionship with persons of a less contemplative type: some finding in extravagant and meaningless gestures an outlet for suppressed vitality; others overflowing with a terrible cheerfulness like "giggling girls and nice japing jugglers"; others so lacking in repose that they "can neither sit still, stand still, nor lie still, unless they be either wagging with their feet or else somewhat doing with their hands." Though he cannot go to the length of condemning these habits as mortal sins, the author of the *Cloud* leaves us in no doubt as to the irritation with which they inspired him, or the distrust with which he regards the spiritual claims of those who fidget.

The attempt to identify this mysterious writer with Walter Hilton, the author of *The Scale of Perfection*, has completely failed: though Hilton's work—especially the exquisite fragment called the *Song of Angels*—certainly betrays his influence. The works attributed to him, if we exclude the translations from

Dionysius and Richard of St. Victor, are only five in number. They are, first, *The Cloud of Unknowing*—the longest and most complete exposition of its author's peculiar doctrine—and, depending from it, four short tracts or letters: *The Epistle of Prayer, The Epistle of Discretion in the Stirrings of the Soul, The Epistle of Privy Counsel,* and *The Treatise of Discerning of Spirits.* Some critics have even disputed the claim of the writer of the *Cloud* to the authorship of these little works, regarding them as the production of a group or school of contemplatives devoted to the study and practice of the Dionysian mystical theology; but the unity of thought and style found in them makes this hypothesis at least improbable. Everything points rather to their being the work of an original mystical genius, of strongly marked character and great literary ability: who, whilst he took the framework of his philosophy from Dionysius the Areopagite, and of his psychology from Richard of St. Victor, yet is in no sense a mere imitator of these masters, but introduced a genuinely new element into mediæval religious literature.

What, then, were his special characteristics? Whence came the fresh colour which he gave to the old Platonic theory of mystical experience? First, I think, from the combination of high spiritual gifts with a vivid sense of humour, keen powers of observation, a robust common-sense: a balance of qualities not indeed rare amongst the mystics, but here presented to us in an extreme form. In his eager gazing on divinity this contemplative never loses touch with humanity, never forgets the sovereign purpose of his writings; which is not a declaration of the spiritual favours he has received, but a helping of his fellow-men to share them. Next, he has a great simplicity of outlook, which enables him to present the result of his highest experiences and intuitions in the most direct and homely language. So actual, and so much a part of his normal existence, are his apprehensions of spiritual reality, that he can give them to us in the plain words of daily life: and thus he is one of the most realistic of mystical writers. He abounds in vivid little phrases—"Call sin a *lump*": "Short prayer pierceth heaven": "Nowhere bodily, is everywhere ghostly": "Who that will not go the strait way to heaven, . . . shall go the soft way to hell." His range of experi-

ence is a wide one. He does not disdain to take a hint from the
wizards and necromancers on the right way to treat the devil; he
draws his illustrations of divine mercy from the homeliest inci-
dents of friendship and parental love. A skilled theologian, quot-
ing St. Augustine and Thomas Aquinas, and using with ease the
language of scholasticism, he is able, on the other hand, to
express the deepest speculations of mystical philosophy without
resorting to academic terminology: as for instance where he
describes the spiritual heaven as a "state" rather than a "place":

"For heaven ghostly is as nigh down as up, and up as down:
behind as before, before as behind, on one side as other.
Insomuch, that whoso had a true desire for to be at heaven, then
that same time he were in heaven ghostly. For the high and the
next way thither is run by desires, and not by paces of feet."

His writings, though they touch on many subjects, are chiefly
concerned with the art of contemplative prayer; that "blind
intent stretching to God" which, if it be wholly set on Him, cannot fail to reach its goal. A peculiar talent for the description and
discrimination of spiritual states has enabled him to discern and
set before us, with astonishing precision and vividness, not only
the strange sensations, the confusion and bewilderment of the
beginner in the early stages of contemplation—the struggle with
distracting thoughts, the silence, the dark—and the unfortunate
state of those theoretical mystics who, "swollen with pride and
with curiosity of much clergy and letterly cunning as in clerks,"
miss that treasure which is "never got by study but all only by
grace"; but also the happiness of those whose "sharp dart of
longing love" has not "failed of the prick, the which is God."

A great simplicity characterises his doctrine of the soul's
attainment of the Absolute. For him there is but one central
necessity: the perfect and passionate setting of the *will* upon the
Divine, so that it is "thy love and thy meaning, the choice and
point of thine heart." Not by deliberate ascetic practices, not by
refusal of the world, not by intellectual striving, but by actively
loving and choosing, by that which a modern psychologist has
called "the synthesis of love and will" does the spirit of man
achieve its goal. "For silence is not God," he says in the *Epistle
of Discretion,* "nor speaking is not God; fasting is not God, nor

eating is not God; loneliness is not God, nor company is not God; nor yet any of all the other two such contraries. He is hid between them, and may not be found by any work of thy soul, but all only by love of thine heart. He may not be known by reason, He may not be gotten by thought, nor concluded by understanding; but He may be loved and chosen with the true lovely will of thine heart. . . . Such a blind shot with the sharp dart of longing love may never fail of the prick, the which is God."

To him who has so loved and chosen, and "in a true will and by an whole intent does purpose him to be a perfect follower of Christ, not only in active living, but in the sovereignest point of contemplative living, the which is possible by grace for to be come to in this present life," these writings are addressed. In the prologue of the *Cloud of Unknowing* we find the warning, so often prefixed to mediæval mystical works, that it shall on no account be lent, given, or read to other men: who could not understand, and might misunderstand in a dangerous sense, its peculiar message. Nor was this warning a mere expression of literary vanity. If we may judge by the examples of possible misunderstanding against which he is careful to guard himself, the almost tiresome reminders that all his remarks are "ghostly, not bodily meant," the standard of intelligence which the author expected from his readers was not a high one. He even fears that some "young presumptuous ghostly disciples" may understand the injunction to "lift up the heart" in a merely physical manner; and either "stare in the stars as if they would be above the moon," or "travail their fleshly hearts outrageously in their breasts" in the effort to make literal "ascensions" to God. Eccentricities of this kind he finds not only foolish but dangerous; they outrage nature, destroy sanity and health, and "hurt full sore the silly soul, and make it fester in fantasy feigned of fiends." He observes with a touch of arrogance that his book is not intended for these undisciplined seekers after the abnormal and the marvellous, nor yet for "fleshly janglers, flatterers and blamers, . . . nor none of these curious, lettered, nor unlearned men." It is to those who feel themselves called to the true prayer of contemplation, to the search for God, whether in the cloister or the world—whose "little secret love" is at once the energising cause of all action, and the hidden sweet savour of life—that he addresses himself. These he instructs in that simple yet difficult art of recollection, the necessary preliminary of any true communion with the spiritual order, in which all sensual images, all memories and thoughts, are as he says, "trodden down under the cloud of forgetting" until "nothing lives in the working mind but a naked intent stretching to God." This "intent stretching"— this loving and vigorous determination of the will—he regards as the central fact of the mystical life; the very heart of effective prayer. Only by its exercise can the spirit, freed from the distractions of memory and sense, focus itself upon Reality and ascend with "a privy love pressed" to that "Cloud of Unknowing"—the Divine Ignorance of the Neoplatonists— wherein is "knit up the ghostly knot of burning love betwixt thee and thy God, in ghostly onehead and according of will."

There is in this doctrine something which should be peculiarly congenial to the activistic tendencies of modern thought. Here is no taint of quietism, no invitation to a spiritual limpness. From first to last glad and deliberate work is demanded of the initiate: an all-round wholeness of experience is insisted on. "A man may not be fully active, but if he be in part contemplative; nor yet fully contemplative, as it may be here, but if he be in part active." Over and over again, the emphasis is laid on this active aspect of all true spirituality—always a favourite theme of the great English mystics. "Love cannot be lazy," said Richard Rolle. So too for the author of the *Cloud* energy is the mark of true affection. "Do forth ever, more and more, so that thou be ever doing. . . . Do on then fast; let see how thou bearest thee. Seest thou not how He standeth and abideth thee?"

True, the will alone, however ardent and industrious, cannot of itself set up communion with the supernal world: this is "the work of only God, specially wrought in what soul that Him liketh." But man can and must do his part. First, there are the virtues to be acquired: those "ornaments of the Spiritual Marriage" with which no mystic can dispense. Since we can but behold that which we are, his character must be set in order, his mind and heart made beautiful and pure, before he can look on the triple star of Goodness, Truth, and Beauty, which is God.

Every great spiritual teacher has spoken in the same sense: of the need for that which Rolle calls the "mending of life"—regeneration, the rebuilding of character—as the preparation of the contemplative act.

For the author of the *Cloud* all human virtue is comprised in the twin qualities of Humility and Charity. He who has these, has all. Humility, in accordance with the doctrine of Richard of St. Victor, he identifies with self-knowledge; the terrible vision of the soul as it is, which induces first self-abasement and then self-purification—the beginning of all spiritual growth, and the necessary antecedent of all knowledge of God. "Therefore swink and sweat in all that thou canst and mayst, for to get thee a true knowing and a feeling of thyself as thou art; and then I trow that soon after that, thou shalt have a true knowing and a feeling of God as He is."

As all man's feeling and thought of himself and his relation to God is comprehended in Humility, so all his feeling and thought of God in Himself is comprehended in Charity; the self-giving love of Divine Perfection "in Himself and for Himself" which Hilton calls "the sovereign and the essential joy." Together these two virtues should embrace the sum of his responses to the Universe; they should govern his attitude to man as well as his attitude to God. "Charity is nought else . . . but love of God for Himself above all creatures, and of man for God even as thyself."

Charity and Humility, then, together with the ardent and industrious will, are the necessary possessions of each soul set upon this adventure. Their presence it is which marks out the true from the false mystic: and it would seem, from the detailed, vivid, and often amusing descriptions of the sanctimonious, the hypocritical, the self-sufficient, and the self-deceived in their "diverse and wonderful variations," that such a test was as greatly needed in the "Ages of Faith" as it is at the present day. Sham spirituality flourished in the mediæval cloister, and offered a constant opportunity of error to those young enthusiasts who were not yet aware that the true freedom of eternity "cometh not with observation." Affectations of sanctity, pretense to rare mystical experiences, were a favourite means of advertisement.

Psychic phenomena, too, seem to have been common: ecstasies, visions, voices, the scent of strange perfumes, the hearing of sweet sounds. For these supposed indications of Divine favour, the author of the *Cloud* has no more respect than the modern psychologist: and here, of course, he is in agreement with all the greatest writers on mysticism, who are unanimous in their dislike and distrust of all visionary and auditive experience. Such things, he considers, are most often hallucination: and, where they are not, should be regarded as the accidents rather than the substance of the contemplative life—the harsh rind of sense, which covers the sweet nut of "pure ghostliness." Were we truly spiritual, we should not need them; for our communion with Reality would then be the direct and ineffable intercourse of like with like.

Moreover, these automatisms are amongst the most dangerous instruments of self-deception. "Ofttimes," he says of those who deliberately seek for revelations, "the devil feigneth quaint sounds in their ears, quaint lights and shining in their eyes, and wonderful smells in their noses: and all is but falsehood." Hence it often happens to those who give themselves up to such experiences, that "fast after such a false feeling, cometh a false knowing in the Fiend's school: . . . for I tell thee truly, that the devil hath his contemplatives, as God hath His." Real spiritual illumination, he thinks, seldom comes by way of these psycho-sensual automatisms "into the body by the windows of our wits." It springs up within the soul in "abundance of ghostly gladness." With so great an authority it comes, bringing with it such wonder and such love, that "he that feeleth it may not have it suspect." But all other abnormal experiences—"comforts, sounds and gladness, and sweetness, that come from without suddenly"—should be set aside, as more often resulting in frenzies and feebleness of spirit than in genuine increase of "ghostly strength."

This healthy and manly view of the mystical life, as a growth towards God, a right employment of the will, rather than a short cut to hidden knowledge or supersensual experience, is one of the strongest characteristics of the writer of the *Cloud;* and constitutes perhaps his greatest claim on our respect. "Mean only xi

God," he says again and again; "Press upon Him with longing love"; "A good *will* is the substance of all perfection." To those who have this good will, he offers his teaching: pointing out the dangers in their way, the errors of mood and of conduct into which they may fall. They are to set about this spiritual work not only with energy, but with *courtesy:* not "snatching as it were a greedy greyhound" at spiritual satisfactions, but gently and joyously pressing towards Him Whom Julian of Norwich called "our most courteous Lord." A glad spirit of dalliance is more becoming to them than the grim determination of the fanatic.

> "Shall I, a gnat which dances in Thy ray,
> *Dare* to be reverent."

Further, he communicates to them certain "ghostly devices" by which they may overcome the inevitable difficulties encountered by beginners in contemplation: the distracting thoughts and memories which torment the self that is struggling to focus all its attention upon the spiritual sphere. The stern repression of such thoughts, however spiritual, he knows to be essential to success: even sin, once it is repented of, must be forgotten in order that Perfect Goodness may be known. The "little word God," and "the little word Love," are the only ideas which may dwell in the contemplative's mind. Anything else splits his attention, and soon proceeds by mental association to lead him further and further from the consideration of that supersensual Reality which he seeks.

The primal need of the purified soul, then, is the power of Concentration. His whole being must be set towards the Object of his craving if he is to attain to it: "Look that *nothing* live in thy working mind, but a naked intent stretching into God." Any thought of Him is inadequate, and for that reason defeats its own end—a doctrine, of course, directly traceable to the "Mystical Theology" of Dionysius the Areopagite. "Of God Himself can no man think," says the writer of the *Cloud,* "And therefore I would leave all that thing that I can think, and choose to my love that thing that I cannot think." The universes which are amenable to the intellect can never satisfy the instincts of the heart.

Further, there is to be no wilful choosing of method: no fussy activity of the surface-intelligence. The mystic who seeks the divine Cloud of Unknowing is to be surrendered to the direction of his deeper mind, his transcendental consciousness: that "spark of the soul" which is in touch with eternal realities. "Meddle thou not therewith, as thou wouldest help it, for dread lest thou spill all. Be thou but the tree, and let it be the wright: be thou but the house, and let it be the husbandman dwelling therein."

In the *Epistle of Privy Counsel* there is a passage which expresses with singular completeness the author's theory of this contemplative art—this silent yet ardent encounter of the soul with God. Prayer, said Mechthild of Magdeburg, brings together two lovers, God and the soul, in a narrow room where they speak much of love: and here the rules which govern that meeting are laid down by a master's hand. "When thou comest by thyself," he says, "think not before what thou shalt do after, but forsake as well good thoughts as evil thoughts, and pray not with thy mouth but list thee right well. And then if thou aught shalt say, look not how much nor how little that it be, nor weigh not what it is nor what it bemeaneth . . . and look that nothing live in thy working mind but a naked intent stretching into God, not clothed in any special thought of God in Himself. . . . This naked intent freely fastened and grounded in very belief shall be nought else to thy thought and to thy feeling but a naked thought and a blind feeling of thine own being: as if thou saidest thus unto God, within in thy meaning, 'That what I am, Lord, I offer unto Thee, without any looking to any quality of Thy Being, but only that Thou art as Thou art, without any more.' That meek darkness be thy mirror, and thy whole remembrance. Think no further of thyself than I bid thee do of thy God, so that thou be one with Him in spirit, as thus without departing and scattering, for He is thy being, and in Him thou art that thou art; not only by cause and by being, but also, He is in thee both thy cause and thy being. And therefore think on God in this work as thou dost on thyself, and on thyself as thou dost on God: that He is as He is and thou art as thou art, and that thy thought be not scattered nor departed, but proved in Him that is All."

The conception of reality which underlies this profound and beautiful passage, has much in common with that found in the work of many other mystics; since it is ultimately derived from the great Neoplatonic philosophy of the contemplative life. But the writer invests it, I think, with a deeper and wider meaning than it is made to bear in the writings even of Ruysbroeck, St. Teresa, or St. John of the Cross. "For He is thy being, and in Him thou art that thou art; not only by cause and by being, but also, He is in thee both thy cause and thy being." It was a deep thinker as well as a great lover who wrote this: one who joined hands with the philosophers, as well as with the saints.

"That meek darkness be thy mirror." What is this darkness? It is the "night of the intellect" into which we are plunged when we attain to a state of consciousness which is above thought; enter on a plane of spiritual experience with which the intellect cannot deal. This is the "Divine Darkness"—the Cloud of Unknowing, or of Ignorance, "dark with excess of light"—preached by Dionysius the Areopagite, and eagerly accepted by his English interpreter. "When I say darkness, I mean a lacking of knowing . . . and for this reason it is not called a cloud of the air, but a cloud of unknowing that is betwixt thee and thy God." It is "a dark mist," he says again, "which seemeth to be between thee and the light thou aspirest to." This dimness and lostness of mind is a paradoxical proof of attainment. Reason is in the dark, because love has entered "the mysterious radiance of the Divine Dark, the inaccessible light wherein the Lord is said to dwell, and to which thought with all its struggles cannot attain."

"Lovers," said Patmore, "put out the candles and draw the curtains, when they wish to see the god and the goddess; and, in the higher communion, the night of thought is the light of perception." These statements cannot be explained: they can only be proved in the experience of the individual soul. "Whoso deserves to see and know God rests therein," says Dionysius of that darkness, "and, by the very fact that he neither sees nor knows, is truly *in* that which surpasses all truth and all knowledge."

"Then," says the writer of the *Cloud*—whispering as it were to the bewildered neophyte the dearest secret of his love—"*then* will He sometimes peradventure send out a beam of ghostly light, piercing this cloud of unknowing that is betwixt thee and Him; and show thee some of His privity, the which man may not, nor cannot speak."

❁   ❁   ❁

Numerous copies of the *Cloud of Unknowing* and the other works attributed to its writer are in existence. Six manuscripts of the *Cloud* are in the British Museum: four on vellum (Harl. 674, Harl. 959, Harl. 2373, and Royal 17 C. xxvi.), all of the 15th century; and two on paper (Royal 17 C. xxvii. of the 16th century, and Royal 17 D. v. late 15th century). All these agree fairly closely; except for the facts that Harl. 2373 is incomplete, several pages having disappeared, and that Harl. 959 gives the substance of the whole work in a slightly shortened form. The present edition is based upon Harl. 674; which has been transcribed and collated with Royal 17 C. xxvi., and in the case of specially obscure passages with Royal 17 C. xxvii., Royal 17 D. v., and Harl. 2373. Obvious errors and omissions have been corrected, and several obscure readings elucidated, from these sources.

The *Cloud of Unknowing* was known, and read, by English Catholics as late as the middle or end of the 17th century. It was much used by the celebrated Benedictine ascetic, the Venerable Augustine Baker (1575–1641), who wrote a long exposition of the doctrine which it contains. Two manuscripts of this treatise exist in the Benedictine College of St. Laurence at Ampleforth; together with a transcript of the *Cloud of Unknowing* dated 1677. Many references to it will also be found in the volume called *Holy Wisdom,* which contains the substances of Augustine Baker's writings on the inner life. The *Cloud* has only once been printed: in 1871, by the Rev. Henry Collins, under the title of *The Divine Cloud,* with a preface and notes attributed to Augustine Baker and probably taken from the treatise mentioned above. This edition is now out of print. The MS. from which it was made is unknown to us. It differs widely, both in the matter of additions and of omissions, from all the texts in the British Museum, and represents a distinctly inferior recension of the work. A mangled rendering of the sublime *Epistle of*

Privy Counsel is prefixed to it. Throughout, the pithy sayings of the original are either misquoted, or expanded into conventional and flavourless sentences. Numerous explanatory phrases for which our manuscripts give no authority have been incorporated into the text. All the quaint and humorous turns of speech are omitted or toned down. The responsibility for these crimes against scholarship cannot now be determined; but it seems likely that the text from which Father Collins' edition was—in his own words—"mostly taken" was a 17th-century paraphrase, made rather in the interests of edification than of accuracy; and that it represents the form in which the work was known and used by Augustine Baker and his contemporaries.

The other works attributed to the author of the *Cloud* have fared better than this. *Dionise Hid Divinite* still remains in MS.: but the *Epistle of Prayer,* the *Epistle of Discretion,* and the *Treatise of Discerning of Spirits,* together with the paraphrase of the *Benjamin Minor* of Richard of St. Victor which is supposed to be by the same hand, were included by Henry Pepwell, in 1521, in a little volume of seven mystical tracts. These are now accessible to the general reader; having been reprinted in the "New Mediæval Library" (1910) under the title of *The Cell of Self-knowledge,* with an admirable introduction and notes by Mr. Edmund Gardner. Mr. Gardner has collated Pepwell's text with that contained in the British Museum manuscript Harl. 674; the same volume which has provided the base-manuscript for the present edition of the *Cloud.*

This edition is intended, not for the student of Middle English, nor for the specialist in mediæval literature; but for the general reader and lover of mysticism. My object has been to produce a readable text, free from learned and critical apparatus. The spelling has therefore been modernised throughout: and except in a few instances, where phrases of a special charm or quaintness, or the alliterative passages so characteristic of the author's style, demanded their retention, obsolete words have been replaced by their nearest modern equivalents. One such word, however, which occurs constantly has generally been retained, on account of its importance and the difficulty of finding an exact substitute for it in current English. This is the verb "to list," with its adjective and adverb "listy" and "listily," and the substantive "list," derived from it. "List" is best understood by comparison with its opposite, "listless." It implies a glad and eager activity, or sometimes an energetic desire or craving: the wish and the will to *do* something. The noun often stands for pleasure or delight, the adverb for the willing and joyous performance of an action: the "putting of one's heart into one's work." The modern "lust," from the same root, suggests a violence which was expressly excluded from the Middle English meaning of "list."

My heartiest thanks are due to Mr. David Inward, who transcribed the manuscript on which this version is based, and throughout has given me skilled and untiring assistance in solving many of the problems which arose in connection with it; and to Mr. J. A. Herbert, Assistant-keeper of Manuscripts in the British Museum, who has read the proofs, and also dated the manuscripts of the *Cloud* for the purposes of the present edition, and to whose expert knowledge and unfailing kindness I owe a deep debt of gratitude.

EVELYN UNDERHILL

Since the Introduction was written there has been published: *The Cloud of Unknowing: The Epistle of Privy Counsel;* and *Denise Hid Divinity.* Anonymous, by a mystic of the 14th century. With Notes on the *Cloud* by Venerable Father Augustine Baker, O.S.B. Edited by Dom Justin McCann, Monk of Ampleforth Abbey.

Glossary

Beholding	Regard, consideration.
Boisterous	Rough, violent, unskilful, crude.
Clergy	Learning.
Con	To know, or be able.
Counsel	Spiritual adviser or director.
Doomsman	Judge.
Even-christian	Neighbour.
Fairhead	Beauty.
Forsobbed	Soaked or penetrated.
Forsunken	Immersed.
Let	To hinder.
Lewd	Unlettered, or ignorant.
Namely	Specially.
Onehead	Union.
Out!	Alas!
Pincher	A covetous or niggardly person.
Ravishing	Ecstasy.
Reckless	Indifferent.
Ronker	A whisperer.
Ronner	A gossip or tale-bearer.
Swink	To labour.
Witting	Knowledge.
Wode	Mad, furious.

Here beginneth a book of contemplation, the which is called the CLOUD OF UNKNOWING, in the which a soul is oned with GOD.

Here Beginneth the Prayer on the Prologue

GOD, unto whom all hearts be open, and unto whom all will speaketh, and unto whom no privy thing is hid. I beseech Thee so for to cleanse the intent of mine heart with the unspeakable gift of Thy grace, that I may perfectly love Thee, and worthily praise Thee. Amen.

Here Beginneth the Prologue

IN THE NAME of the Father and of the Son and of the Holy Ghost! I charge thee and I beseech thee, with as much power and virtue as the bond of charity is sufficient to suffer, whatsoever thou be that this book shalt have in possession, either by property, either by keeping, by bearing as messenger, or else by borrowing, that in as much as in thee is by will and advisement, neither thou read it, nor write it, nor speak it, nor yet suffer it be read, written, or spoken, of any or to any but if it be of such one, or to such one, that hath by thy supposing in a true will and by an whole intent purposed him to be a perfect follower of Christ not only in active living, but in the sovereignest point of contemplative living the which is possible by grace for to be come to in this present life of a perfect soul yet abiding in this deadly body; and thereto that doth that in him is, and by thy supposing hath done long time before, for to able him to contemplative living by the virtuous means of active living. For else it accordeth nothing to him. And over this I charge thee and I beseech thee by the authority of charity, that if any such shall read it, write it, or speak it, or else hear it be read or spoken, that thou charge him as I do thee, for to take him time to read it, speak it, write it, or hear it, all over. For peradventure there is some matter therein in the beginning or in the middle, the which is hanging, and not fully declared where it standeth: and if it be not there, it is soon after, or else in the end. Wherefore if a man saw one matter and not another, peradventure he might lightly be led into error; and therefore in eschewing of this error, both in thyself and in all other, I pray thee for charity do as I say thee.

Fleshly janglers, open praisers and blamers of themselves or of any other, tellers of trifles, ronners and tattlers of tales, and all manner of pinchers, cared I never that they saw this book. For mine intent was never to write such thing unto them, and therefore I would that they meddle not therewith; neither they, nor any of these curious, lettered, or unlearned men. Yea, although that they be full good men of active living, yet this matter accordeth nothing to them. But if it be to those men, the which although they stand in activity by outward form of living, nevertheless yet by inward stirring after the privy spirit of God, whose dooms be hid, they be full graciously disposed, not continually as it is proper to very contemplatives, but now and then to be perceivers in the highest point of this contemplative act; if such men might see it, they should by the grace of God be greatly comforted thereby.

This book is distinguished in seventy chapters and five. Of the which chapters, the last chapter of all teacheth some certain tokens by the which a soul may verily prove whether he be called of God to be a worker in this work or none.

Here Beginneth
a Table of the Chapters

AND HERE ENDETH THE TABLE OF THE CHAPTERS

GHOSTLY FRIEND IN GOD, I pray thee and I beseech thee that thou wilt have a busy beholding to the course and the manner of thy calling. And thank God heartily so that thou mayest through help of His grace stand stiffly in the state, in the degree, and in the form of living that thou hast entirely purposed against all the subtle assailing of thy bodily and ghostly enemies, and win to the crown of life that evermore lasteth. Amen.

Here Beginneth the First Chapter

Of four degrees of Christian men's living; and of the course of his calling that this book was made unto.

Ghostly friend in God, thou shalt well understand that I find, in my boisterous beholding, four degrees and forms of Christian men's living: and they be these, Common, Special, Singular, and Perfect. Three of these may be begun and ended in this life; and the fourth may by grace be begun here, but it shall ever last without end in the bliss of Heaven. And right as thou seest how they be set here in order each one after other; first Common, then Special, after Singular, and last Perfect, right so me thinketh that in the same order and in the same course our Lord hath of His great mercy called thee and led thee unto Him by the desire of thine heart. For first thou wottest well that when thou wert living in the common degree of Christian men's living in company of thy worldly friends, it seemeth to me that the everlasting love of His Godhead, through the which He made thee and wrought thee when thou wert nought, and sithen bought thee with the price of His precious blood when thou wert lost in Adam, might not suffer thee to be so far from Him in form and degree of living. And therefore He kindled thy desire full graciously, and fastened by it a leash of longing, and led thee by it into a more special state and form of living, to be a servant among the special servants of His; where thou mightest learn to live more specially and more ghostly in His service than thou didst, or mightest do, in the common degree of living before. And what more?

Yet it seemeth that He would not leave thee thus lightly, for love of His heart, the which He hath evermore had unto thee

1

since thou wert aught: but what did He? Seest thou nought how listily and how graciously He hath privily pulled thee to the third degree and manner of living, the which is called Singular? In the which solitary form and manner of living, thou mayest learn to lift up the foot of thy love; and step towards that state and degree of living that is perfect, and the last state of all.

Here Beginneth the Second Chapter

A short stirring to meekness, and to the work of this book.

Look up now, weak wretch, and see what thou art. What art thou, and what hast thou merited, thus to be called of our Lord? What weary wretched heart, and sleeping in sloth, is that, the which is not wakened with the draught of this love and the voice of this calling! Beware, thou wretch, in this while with thine enemy; and hold thee never the holier nor the better, for the worthiness of this calling and for the singular form of living that thou art in. But the more wretched and cursed, unless thou do that in thee is goodly, by grace and by counsel, to live after thy calling. And insomuch thou shouldest be more meek and loving to thy ghostly spouse, that He that is the Almighty God, King of Kings and Lord of Lords, would meek Him so low unto thee, and amongst all the flock of His sheep so graciously would choose thee to be one of His specials, and sithen set thee in the place of pasture, where thou mayest be fed with the sweetness of His love, in earnest of thine heritage the Kingdom of Heaven.

Do on then, I pray thee, fast. Look now forwards and let be backwards; and see what thee faileth, and not what thou hast, for that is the readiest getting and keeping of meekness. All thy life now behoveth altogether to stand in desire, if thou shalt profit in degree of perfection. This desire behoveth altogether be wrought in thy will, by the hand of Almighty God and thy consent. But one thing I tell thee. He is a jealous lover and suffereth no fellowship, and Him list not work in thy will but if He be only with thee by Himself. He asketh none help, but only

3

thyself. He wills, thou do but look on Him and let Him alone. And keep thou the windows and the door, for flies and enemies assailing. And if thou be willing to do this, thee needeth but meekly press upon Him with prayer, and soon will He help thee. Press on then, let see how thou bearest thee. He is full ready, and doth but abideth thee. But what shalt thou do, and how shalt thou press?

Here Beginneth the Third Chapter

How the work of this book shall be wrought, and of the worthiness of it before all other works.

Lift up thine heart unto God with a meek stirring of love; and mean Himself, and none of His goods. And thereto, look thee loath to think on aught but Himself. So that nought work in thy wit, nor in thy will, but only Himself. And do that in thee is to forget all the creatures that ever God made and the works of them; so that thy thought nor thy desire be not directed nor stretched to any of them, neither in general nor in special, but let them be, and take no heed to them. This is the work of the soul that most pleaseth God. All saints and angels have joy of this work, and hasten them to help it in all their might. All fiends be furious when thou thus dost, and try for to defeat it in all that they can. All men living in earth be wonderfully holpen of this work, thou wottest not how. Yea, the souls in purgatory be eased of their pain by virtue of this work. Thyself art cleansed and made virtuous by no work so much. And yet it is the lightest work of all, when a soul is helped with grace in sensible list, and soonest done. But else it is hard, and wonderful to thee for to do.

Let not, therefore, but travail therein till thou feel list. For at the first time when thou dost it, thou findest but a darkness; and as it were a cloud of unknowing, thou knowest not what, saving that thou feelest in thy will a naked intent unto God. This darkness and this cloud is, howsoever thou dost, betwixt thee and thy God, and letteth thee that thou mayest neither see Him clearly by light of understanding in thy reason, nor feel Him in sweetness of love in thine affection. And therefore shape thee to bide in this darkness as long as thou mayest, evermore crying after Him that thou lovest. For if ever thou shalt feel Him or see Him, as it may be here, it behoveth always to be in this cloud in this darkness. And if thou wilt busily travail as I bid thee, I trust in His mercy that thou shalt come thereto.

Here Beginneth the Fourth Chapter

Of the shortness of this work, and how it may not be come to by curiosity of wit, nor by imagination.

But for this, that thou shalt not err in this working and ween that it be otherwise than it is, I shall tell thee a little more thereof, as me thinketh.

This work asketh no long time or it be once truly done, as some men ween; for it is the shortest work of all that man may imagine. It is never longer, nor shorter, than is an atom: the which atom, by the definition of true philosophers in the science of astronomy, is the least part of time. And it is so little that for the littleness of it, it is indivisible and nearly incomprehensible. This is that time of the which it is written: All time that is given to thee, it shall be asked of thee, how thou hast dispended it. And reasonable thing it is that thou give account of it: for it is neither longer nor shorter, but even according to one only stirring that is within the principal working might of thy soul, the which is thy will. For even so many willings or desirings, and no more nor no fewer, may be and are in one hour in thy will, as are atoms in one hour. And if thou wert reformed by grace to the first state of man's soul, as it was before sin, then thou shouldest evermore by help of that grace be lord of that stirring or of those stirrings. So that none went forby, but all they should stretch into the sovereign desirable, and into the highest willable thing: the which is God. For He is even meet to our soul by measuring of His Godhead; and our soul even meet unto Him by worthiness of our creation to His image and to His likeness. And He

7

by Himself without more, and none but He, is sufficient to the
full and much more to fulfil the will and the desire of our soul.
And our soul by virtue of this reforming grace is made sufficient
to the full to comprehend all Him by love, the which is incomprehensible to all created knowledgeable powers, as is angel, or
man's soul; I mean, by their knowing, and not by their loving.
And therefore I call them in this case knowledgeable powers.
But yet all reasonable creatures, angel and man, have in them
each one by himself, one principal working power, the which is
called a knowledgeable power, and another principal working
power, the which is called a loving power. Of the which two
powers, to the first, the which is a knowledgeable power, God
that is the maker of them is evermore incomprehensible; and to
the second, the which is the loving power, in each one diversely
He is all comprehensible to the full. Insomuch that a loving soul
alone in itself, by virtue of love should comprehend in itself Him
that is sufficient to the full—and much more, without comparison—to fill all the souls and angels that ever may be. And this is
the endless marvellous miracle of love; the working of which
shall never take end, for ever shall He do it, and never shall He
cease for to do it. See who by grace see may, for the feeling of
this is endless bliss, and the contrary is endless pain.

And therefore whoso were reformed by grace thus to continue in keeping of the stirrings of his will, should never be in
this life—as he may not be without these stirrings in nature—
without some taste of the endless sweetness, and in the bliss of
heaven without the full food. And therefore have no wonder
though I stir thee to this work. For this is the work, as thou shalt
hear afterward, in the which man should have continued if he
never had sinned: and to the which working man was made, and
all things for man, to help him and further him thereto, and by
the which working a man shall be repaired again. And for the
defailing of this working, a man falleth evermore deeper and
deeper in sin, and further and further from God. And by keeping and continual working in this work only without more, a man
evermore riseth higher and higher from sin, and nearer and
nearer unto God.

And therefore take good heed unto time, how that thou

dispendest it: for nothing is more precious than time. In one little time, as little as it is, may heaven be won and lost. A token it
is that time is precious: for God, that is given of time, giveth
never two times together, but each one after other. And this He
doth, for He will not reverse the order or the ordinal course in
the cause of His creation. For time is made for man, and not
man for time. And therefore God, that is the ruler of nature, will
not in His giving of time go before the stirring of nature in man's
soul; the which is even according to one time only. So that man
shall have none excusation against God in the Doom, and at the
giving of account of dispending of time, saying, "Thou givest two
times at once, and I have but one stirring at once."

But sorrowfully thou sayest now, "How shall I do? and sith
this is thus that thou sayest, how shall I give account of each
time severally; I that have unto this day, now of four and twen-
ty years age, never took heed of time? If I would now amend it,
thou wottest well, by very reason of thy words written before, it
may not be after the course of nature, nor of common grace,
that I should now heed or else make satisfaction, for any more
times than for those that be for to come. Yea, and moreover well
I wot by very proof, that of those that be to come I shall on no
wise, for abundance of frailty and slowness of spirits, be able to
observe one of an hundred. So that I am verily concluded in
these reasons. Help me now for the love of JESUS!"

Right well hast thou said, for the love of JESUS. For in the
love of JESUS; there shall be thine help. Love is such a power,
that it maketh all thing common. Love therefore JESUS; and all
thing that He hath, it is thine. He by His Godhead is maker and
giver of time. He by His manhood is the very keeper of time.
And He by His Godhead and His manhood together, is the
truest Doomsman, and the asker of account of dispending of
time. Knit thee therefore to Him, by love and by belief, and
then by virtue of that knot thou shalt be common perceiver with
Him, and with all that by love so be knitted unto Him: that is to
say, with our Lady Saint Mary that full was of all grace in keeping of time, with all the angels of heaven that never may lose
time, and with all the saints in heaven and in earth, that by the
grace of JESUS heed time full justly in virtue of love. Lo! here

lieth comfort; construe thou clearly, and pick thee some profit. But of one thing I warn thee amongst all other. I cannot see who may truly challenge community thus with JESUS and His just Mother, His high angels and also with His saints; but if he be such an one, that doth that in him is with helping of grace in keeping of time. So that he be seen to be a profiter on his part, so little as is, unto the community; as each one of them doth on his.

And therefore take heed to this work, and to the marvellous manner of it within in thy soul. For if it be truly conceived, it is but a sudden stirring, and as it were unadvised, speedily spring-ing unto God as a sparkle from the coal. And it is marvellous to number the stirrings that may be in one hour wrought in a soul that is disposed to this work. And yet in one stirring of all these, he may have suddenly and perfectly forgotten all created thing. But fast after each stirring, for corruption of the flesh, it falleth down again to some thought or to some done or undone deed. But what thereof? For fast after, it riseth again as suddenly as it did before.

And here may men shortly conceive the manner of this work-ing, and clearly know that it is far from any fantasy, or any false imagination or quaint opinion: the which be brought in, not by such a devout and a meek blind stirring of love, but by a proud, curious, and an imaginative wit. Such a proud, curious wit behoveth always be borne down and stiffly trodden down under foot, if this work shall truly be conceived in purity of spirit. For whoso heareth this work either be read or spoken, of, and weeneth that it may, or should be come to by travail in their wits, and therefore they sit and seek in their wits how that it may be, and in this curiosity they travail their imagination peradventure against the course of nature, and they feign a manner of work-ing the which is neither bodily nor ghostly—truly this man, whatsoever he be, is perilously deceived. Insomuch, that unless God of His great goodness shew His merciful miracle, and make him soon to leave work, and meek him to counsel of proved workers, he shall fall either into frenzies, or else into other great mischiefs of ghostly sins and devils' deceits; through the which he may lightly be lost, both life and soul, without any end. And therefore for God's love be wary in this work, and travail not in thy wits nor in thy imagination on nowise: for I tell thee truly, it may not be come to by travail in them, and therefore leave them and work not with them.

And ween not, for I call it a darkness or a cloud, that it be any cloud congealed of the humours that flee in the air, nor yet any darkness such as is in thine house on nights when the candle is out. For such a darkness and such a cloud mayest thou imagine with curiosity of wit, for to bear before thine eyes in the lightest day of summer: and also contrariwise in the darkest night of winter, thou mayest imagine a clear shining light. Let be such falsehood. I mean not thus. For when I say darkness, I mean a lacking of knowing: as all that thing that thou knowest not, or else that thou hast forgotten, it is dark to thee; for thou seest it not with thy ghostly eye. And for this reason it is not called a cloud of the air, but a cloud of unknowing, that is betwixt thee and thy God.

Here Beginneth the Fifth Chapter

That in the time of this work all the creatures that ever have been, be now, or ever shall be, and all the works of those same creatures, should be hid under the cloud of forgetting.

And if ever thou shalt come to this cloud and dwell and work therein as I bid thee, thee behoveth as this cloud of unknowing is above thee, betwixt thee and thy God, right so put a cloud of forgetting beneath thee; betwixt thee and all the creatures that ever be made. Thee thinketh, peradventure, that thou art full far from God because that this cloud of unknowing is betwixt thee and thy God: but surely, an it be well conceived, thou art well further from Him when thou hast no cloud of forgetting betwixt thee and all the creatures that ever be made. As oft as I say, all the creatures that ever be made, as oft I mean not only the creatures themselves, but also all the works and the conditions of the same creatures. I take out not one creature, whether they be bodily creatures or ghostly, nor yet any condition or work of any creature, whether they be good or evil: but shortly to say, all should be hid under the cloud of forgetting in this case.

For although it be full profitable sometime to think of certain conditions and deeds of some certain special creatures, nevertheless yet in this work it profiteth little or nought. For why? Memory or thinking of any creature that ever God made, or of any of their deeds either, it is a manner of ghostly light: for the eye of thy soul is opened on it and even fixed thereupon, as the eye of a shooter is upon the prick that he shooteth to. And one thing I tell thee, that all thing that thou thinketh upon, it is above thee for the time, and betwixt thee and thy God: and insomuch thou art the further from God, that aught is in thy mind but only God.

Yea! and, if it be courteous and seemly to say, in this work it profiteth little or nought to think of the kindness or the worthiness of God, nor on our Lady, nor on the saints or angels in heaven, nor yet on the joys in heaven: that is to say, with a special beholding to them, as thou wouldest by that beholding feed and increase thy purpose. I trow that on nowise it should help in this case and in this work. For although it be good to think upon the kindness of God, and to love Him and praise Him for it, yet it is far better to think upon the naked being of Him, and to love Him and praise Him for Himself.

Here Beginneth the Sixth Chapter

A short conceit of the work of this book, treated by question.

B ut now thou askest me and sayest, "How shall I think on Himself, and what is He?" and to this I cannot answer thee but this: "I wot not."

For thou hast brought me with thy question into that same darkness, and into that same cloud of unknowing, that I would thou wert in thyself. For of all other creatures and their works, yea, and of the works of God's self, may a man through grace have fullhead of knowing, and well he can think of them: but of God Himself can no man think. And therefore I would leave all that thing that I can think, and choose to my love that thing that I cannot think. For why; He may well be loved, but not thought. By love may He be gotten and holden; but by thought never. And therefore, although it be good sometime to think of the kindness and the worthiness of God in special, and although it be a light and a part of contemplation: nevertheless yet in this work it shall be cast down and covered with a cloud of forgetting. And thou shalt step above it stalwartly, but listily, with a devout and a pleasing stirring of love, and try for to pierce that darkness above thee. And smite upon that thick cloud of unknowing with a sharp dart of longing love; and go not thence for thing that befalleth.

Here Beginneth the Seventh Chapter

How a man shall have him in this work against all thoughts, and specially against all those that arise of his own curiosity, of cunning, and of natural wit.

And if any thought rise and will press continually above thee betwixt thee and that darkness, and ask thee saying, "What seekest thou, and what wouldest thou have?" say thou, that it is God that thou wouldest have. "Him I covet, Him I seek, and nought but Him."

And if he ask thee, "What is that God?" say thou, that it is God that made thee and bought thee, and that graciously hath called thee to thy degree. "And in Him," say, "thou hast no skill." And therefore say, "Go thou down again," and tread him fast down with a stirring of love, although he seem to thee right holy, and seem to thee as he would help thee to seek Him. For peradventure he will bring to thy mind diverse full fair and wonderful points of His kindness, and say that He is full sweet, and full loving, full gracious, and full merciful. And if thou wilt hear him, he coveteth no better; for at the last he will thus jangle ever more and more till he bring thee lower, to the mind of His Passion.

And there will he let thee see the wonderful kindness of God, and if thou hear him, he careth for nought better. For soon after he will let thee see thine old wretched living, and peradventure in seeing and thinking thereof he will bring to thy mind some place that thou hast dwelt in before this time. So that at the last, or ever thou wit, thou shalt be scattered thou wottest not where. The cause of this scattering is, that thou heardest him first wilfully, then answeredest him, receivedest him, and lettest him alone.

And yet, nevertheless, the thing that he said was both good

and holy. Yea, and so holy, that what man or woman that weeneth to come to contemplation without many such sweet meditations of their own wretchedness, the passion, the kindness, and the great goodness, and the worthiness of God coming before, surely he shall err and fail of his purpose. And yet, nevertheless, it behoveth a man or a woman that hath long time been used in these meditations, nevertheless to leave them, and put them and hold them far down under the cloud of forgetting, if ever he shall pierce the cloud of unknowing betwixt him and his God. Therefore what time that thou purposest thee to this work, and feelest by grace that thou art called of God, lift then up thine heart unto God with a meek stirring of love; and mean God that made thee, and bought thee, and that graciously hath called thee to thy degree, and receive none other thought of God. And yet not all these, but if thou list; for it sufficeth enough, a naked intent direct unto God without any other cause than Himself.

And if thee list have this intent lapped and folden in one word, for thou shouldest have better hold thereupon, take thee but a little word of one syllable: for so it is better than of two, for ever the shorter it is the better it accordeth with the work of the Spirit. And such a word is this word GOD or this word LOVE. Choose thee whether thou wilt, or another; as thee list, which that thee liketh best of one syllable. And fasten this word to thine heart, so that it never go thence for thing that befalleth.

This word shall be thy shield and thy spear, whether thou ridest on peace or on war. With this word, thou shalt beat on this cloud and this darkness above thee. With this word, thou shalt smite down all manner of thought under the cloud of forgetting. Insomuch, that if any thought press upon thee to ask thee what thou wouldest have, answer them with no more words but with this one word. And if he proffer thee of his great clergy to expound thee that word and to tell thee the conditions of that word, say him: That thou wilt have it all whole, and not broken nor undone. And if thou wilt hold thee fast on this purpose, be thou sure, he will no while abide. And why? For that thou wilt not let him feed him on such sweet meditations of God touched before.

Here Beginneth the Eighth Chapter

A good declaring of certain doubts that may fall in this work, treated by question, in destroying of a man's own curiosity, of cunning, and of natural wit, and in distinguishing of the degrees and the parts of active living and contemplative.

But now thou askest me, "What is he, this that thus presseth upon me in this work; and whether it is a good thing or an evil? And if it be an evil thing, then have I marvel," thou sayest, "why that he will increase a man's devotion so much. For sometimes me think that it is a passing comfort to listen after his tales. For he will sometime, me think, make me weep full heartily for pity of the Passion of Christ, sometime for my wretchedness, and for many other reasons, that me thinketh be full holy, and that done me much good. And therefore me thinketh that he should on nowise be evil; and if he be good, and with his sweet tales doth me so much good withal, then I have great marvel why that thou biddest me put him down and away so far under the cloud of forgetting?"

Now surely me thinketh that this is a well moved question, and therefore I think to answer thereto so feebly as I can. First when thou askest me what is he, this that presseth so fast upon thee in this work, proffering to help thee in this work; I say that it is a sharp and a clear beholding of thy natural wit, printed in thy reason within in thy soul. And where thou askest me thereof whether it be good or evil, I say that it behoveth always be good in its nature. For why, it is a beam of the likeness of God. But the use thereof may be both good and evil. Good, when it is opened by grace for to see thy wretchedness, the passion, the kindness, and the wonderful works of God in His creatures bodily and ghostly. And then it is no wonder though it increase thy devotion full much, as thou sayest. But then is the use evil, when it is swollen with pride and with curiosity of much clergy and letterly cunning as in clerks; and maketh them press for to be holden not meek scholars and masters of divinity or of devotion, but proud scholars of the devil and masters of vanity and of falsehood. And in other men or women whatso they be, religious or seculars, the use and the working of this natural wit is then evil, when it is swollen with proud and curious skills of worldly things, and fleshly conceits in coveting of worldly worships and having of riches and vain plesaunce and flatterings of others.

And where that thou askest me, why that thou shalt put it down under the cloud of forgetting, since it is so, that it is good in its nature, and thereto when it is well used it doth thee so much good and increaseth thy devotion so much. To this I answer and say—That thou shalt well understand that there be two manner of lives in Holy Church. The one is active life, and the other is contemplative life. Active is the lower, and contemplative is the higher. Active life hath two degrees, a higher and a lower: and also contemplative life hath two degrees, a lower and a higher. Also, these two lives be so coupled together that although they be divers in some part, yet neither of them may be had fully without some part of the other. For why? That part that is the higher part of active life, that same part is the lower part of contemplative life. So that a man may not be fully active, but if he be in part contemplative; nor yet fully contemplative, as it may be here, but if he be in part active. The condition of active life is such, that it is both begun and ended in this life; but not so of contemplative life. For it is begun in this life, and shall last without end. For why? That part that Mary chose shall never be taken away. Active life is troubled and travailed about many things; but contemplative sitteth in peace with one thing.

The lower part of active life standeth in good and honest bodily works of mercy and of charity. The higher part of active life and the lower part of contemplative life lieth in goodly ghostly meditations, and busy beholding unto a man's own wretchedness with sorrow and contrition, unto the Passion of Christ and of His servants with pity and compassion, and unto the wonderful gifts,

kindness, and works of God in all His creatures bodily and ghostly with thanking and praising. But the higher part of contemplation, as it may be had here, hangeth all wholly in this darkness
and in this cloud of unknowing; with a loving stirring and a blind
beholding unto the naked being of God Himself only.

In the lower part of active life a man is without himself and
beneath himself. In the higher part of active life and the lower
part of contemplative life, a man is within himself and even with
himself. But in the higher part of contemplative life, a man is
above himself and under his God. Above himself he is: for why,
he purposeth him to win thither by grace, whither he may not
come by nature. That is to say, to be knit to God in spirit, and in
onehead of love and accordance of will. And right as it is impossible, to man's understanding, for a man to come to the higher
part of active life, but if he cease for a time of the lower part; so
it is that a man shall not come to the higher part of contemplative life, but if he cease for a time of the lower part. And as
unlawful a thing as it is, and as much as it would let a man that
sat in his meditations, to have regard then to his outward bodily works, the which he had done, or else should do, although
they were never so holy works in themselves: surely as unlikely
a thing it is, and as much would it let a man that should work in
this darkness and in this cloud of unknowing with an affectuous
stirring of love to God for Himself, for to let any thought or any
meditation of God's wonderful gifts, kindness, and works in any
of His creatures bodily or ghostly, rise upon him to press betwixt
him and his God; although they be never so holy thoughts, nor
so profound, nor so comfortable.

And for this reason it is that I bid thee put down such a sharp
subtle thought, and cover him with a thick cloud of forgetting,
be he never so holy nor promise he thee never so well for to help
thee in thy purpose. For why, love may reach to God in this life,
but not knowing. And all the whiles that the soul dwelleth in this
deadly body, evermore is the sharpness of our understanding in
beholding of all ghostly things, but most specially of God,
mingled with some manner of fantasy; for the which our work
should be unclean. And unless more wonder were, it should
lead us into much error.

Here Beginneth the Ninth Chapter

That in the time of this work the remembrance of the holiest creature that ever God made letteth more than it profiteth.

A nd therefore the sharp stirring of thine understanding, that will always press upon thee when thou settest thee to this work, behoveth always be borne down; and but thou bear him down, he will bear thee down. Insomuch, that when thou weenest best to abide in this darkness, and that nought is in thy mind but only God; an thou look truly thou shalt find thy mind not occupied in this darkness, but in a clear beholding of some thing beneath God. And if it thus be, surely then is that thing above thee for the time, and betwixt thee and thy God. And therefore purpose thee to put down such clear beholdings, be they never so holy nor so likely. For one thing I tell thee, it is more profitable to the health of thy soul, more worthy in itself, and more pleasing to God and to all the saints and angels in heaven—yea, and more helpful to all thy friends, bodily and ghostly, quick and dead—such a blind stirring of love unto God for Himself, and such a privy pressing upon this cloud of unknowing, and better thee were for to have it and for to feel it in thine affection ghostly, than it is for to have the eyes of thy soul opened in contemplation or beholding of all the angels or saints in heaven, or in hearing of all the mirth and the melody that is amongst them in bliss.

And look thou have no wonder of this: for mightest thou once see it as clearly, as thou mayest by grace come to for to grope it and feel it in this life, thou wouldest think as I say. But be thou

sure that clear sight shall never man have here in this life: but
the feeling may men have through grace when God vouchsafeth. And therefore lift up thy love to that cloud: rather, if I
shall say thee sooth, let God draw thy love up to that cloud and
strive thou through help of His grace to forget all other thing.

For since a naked remembrance of any thing under God
pressing against thy will and thy witting putteth thee farther
from God than thou shouldest be if it were not, and letteth thee,
and maketh thee inasmuch more unable to feel in experience
the fruit of His love, what trowest thou then that a remembrance wittingly and wilfully drawn upon thee will hinder thee
in thy purpose? And since a remembrance of any special saint or
of any clean ghostly thing will hinder thee so much, what trowest thou then that the remembrance of any man living in this
wretched life, or of any manner of bodily or worldly thing, will
hinder thee and let thee in this work?

I say not that such a naked sudden thought of any good and
clean ghostly thing under God pressing against thy will or thy
witting, or else wilfully drawn upon thee with advisement in
increasing of thy devotion, although it be letting to this manner
of work—that it is therefore evil. Nay! God forbid that thou take
it so. But I say, although it be good and holy, yet in this work it
letteth more than it profiteth. I mean for the time. For why?
Surely he that seeketh God perfectly, he will not rest him finally
in the remembrance of any angel or saint that is in heaven.

Here Beginneth the Tenth Chapter

How a man shall know when his thought is no sin; and if it be sin, when it is deadly and when it is venial.

But it is not thus of the remembrance of any man or woman living in this life, or of any bodily or worldly thing whatsoever that it be. For why, a naked sudden thought of any of them, pressing against thy will and thy witting, although it be no sin imputed unto thee—for it is the pain of the original sin pressing against thy power, of the which sin thou art cleansed in thy baptism—nevertheless yet if this sudden stirring or thought be not smitten soon down, as fast for frailty thy fleshly heart is strained thereby: with some manner of liking, if it be a thing that pleaseth thee or hath pleased thee before, or else with some manner of grumbling, if it be a thing that thee think grieveth thee, or hath grieved thee before. The which fastening, although it may in fleshly living men and women that be in deadly sin before be deadly; nevertheless in thee and in all other that have in a true will forsaken the world, and are obliged unto any degree in devout living in Holy Church, what so it be, privy or open, and thereto that will be ruled not after their own will and their own wit, but after the will and the counsel of their sovereigns, what so they be, religious or seculars, such a liking or a grumbling fastened in the fleshly heart is but venial sin. The cause of this is the grounding and the rooting of your intent in God, made in the beginning of your living in that state that ye stand in, by the witness and the counsel of some discreet father.

But if it so be, that this liking or grumbling fastened in thy fleshly heart be suffered so long to abide unreproved, that then at the last it is fastened to the ghostly heart, that is to say the will, with a full consent: then, it is deadly sin. And this befalleth when thou or any of them that I speak of wilfully draw upon thee the remembrance of any man or woman living in this life, or of any bodily or worldly thing other: insomuch, that if it be a thing the which grieveth or hath grieved thee before, there riseth in thee an angry passion and an appetite of vengeance, the which is called Wrath. Or else a fell disdain and a manner of loathsomeness of their person, with despiteful and condemning thoughts, the which is called Envy. Or else a weariness and an unlistiness of any good occupation bodily or ghostly, the which is called Sloth.

And if it be a thing that pleaseth thee, or hath pleased thee before, there riseth in thee a passing delight for to think on that thing what so it be. Insomuch, that thou restest thee in that thought, and finally fastenest thine heart and thy will thereto, and feedest thy fleshly heart therewith: so that thee think for the time that thou covetest none other wealth, but to live ever in such a peace and rest with that thing that thou thinkest upon. If this thought that thou thus drawest upon thee, or else receivest when it is put unto thee, and that thou restest thee thus in with delight, be worthiness of nature or of knowing, of grace or of degree, of favour or of fairhead, then it is Pride. And if it be any manner of worldly good, riches or chattels, or what that man may have or be lord of, then it is Covetyse. If it be dainty meats and drinks, or any manner of delights that man may taste, then it is Gluttony. And if it be love or plesaunce, or any manner of fleshly dalliance, glosing or flattering of any man or woman living in this life, or of thyself either: then it is Lechery.

Here Beginneth the Eleventh Chapter

That a man should weigh each thought and each stirring after that it is, and always eschew recklessness in venial sin.

I say not this for that I trow that thou, or any other such as I speak of, be guilty and cumbered with any such sins; but for that I would that thou weighest each thought and each stirring after that it is, and for I would that thou travailedst busily to destroy the first stirring and thought of these things that thou mayest thus sin in. For one thing I tell thee; that who weigheth not, or setteth little by, the first thought—yea, although it be no sin unto him—that he, whosoever that he be, shall not eschew recklessness in venial sin. Venial sin shall no man utterly eschew in this deadly life. But recklessness in venial sin should always be eschewed of all the true disciples of perfection; and else I have no wonder though they soon sin deadly.

Here Beginneth the Twelfth Chapter

That by virtue of this work sin is not only destroyed, but also virtues begotten.

And, therefore, if thou wilt stand and not fall, cease never in thine intent: but beat evermore on this cloud of unknowing that is betwixt thee and thy God with a sharp dart of longing love, and loathe for to think on aught under God, and go not thence for anything that befalleth. For this is only by itself that work that destroyeth the ground and the root of sin. Fast thou never so much, wake thou never so long, rise thou never so early, lie thou never so hard, wear thou never so sharp; yea, and if it were lawful to do—as it is not—put thou out thine eyes, cut thou out thy tongue of thy mouth, stop thou thine ears and thy nose never so fast, though thou shear away thy members, and do all the pain to thy body that thou mayest or canst think: all this would help thee right nought. Yet will stirring and rising of sin be in thee.

Yea, and what more? Weep thou never so much for sorrow of thy sins, or of the Passion of Christ, or have thou never so much mind of the joys of heaven, what may it do to thee? Surely much good, much help, much profit, and much grace will it get thee. But in comparison of this blind stirring of love, it is but a little that it doth, or may do, without this. This by itself is the best part of Mary without these other. They without it profit but little or nought. It destroyeth not only the ground and the root of sin as it may be here, but thereto it getteth virtues. For an it be truly conceived, all virtues shall truly be, and perfectly conceived, and feelingly comprehended, in it, without any mingling of the intent. And have a man never so many virtues without it, all they be mingled with some crooked intent, for the which they be imperfect.

For virtue is nought else but an ordained and a measured affection, plainly directed unto God for Himself. For why? He in Himself is the pure cause of all virtues: insomuch, that if any man be stirred to any one virtue by any other cause mingled with Him, yea, although that He be the chief, yet that virtue is then imperfect. As thus by example may be seen in one virtue or two instead of all the other; and well may these two virtues be meekness and charity. For whoso might get these two clearly, him needeth no more: for why, he hath all.

Here Beginneth
the Thirteenth Chapter

What meekness is in itself, and when it is perfect and when it is imperfect.

Now let see first of the virtue of meekness; how that it is imperfect when it is caused of any other thing mingled with God although He be the chief; and how that it is perfect when it is caused of God by Himself. And first it is to wit, what meekness is in itself, if this matter shall clearly be seen and conceived; and thereafter may it more verily be conceived in truth of spirit what is the cause thereof.

Meekness in itself is nought else, but a true knowing and feeling of a man's self as he is. For surely whoso might verily see and feel himself as he is, he should verily be meek. Two things there be, the which be cause of this meekness; the which be these. One is the filth, the wretchedness, and the frailty of man, into the which he is fallen by sin; and the which always him behoveth to feel in some part the whiles he liveth in this life, be he never so holy. Another is the over-abundant love and the worthiness of God in Himself; in beholding of the which all nature quaketh, all clerks be fools, and all saints and angels be blind. Insomuch, that were it not that through the wisdom of His Godhead He measured their beholding after their ableness in nature and in grace, I defail to say what should befall them.

This second cause is perfect; for why, it shall last without end. And the tother before is imperfect; for why, it shall not only fail at the end of this life, but full oft it may befall that a soul in this deadly body for abundance of grace in multiplying of his desire—as oft and as long as God vouchsafeth for to work it— shall have suddenly and perfectly lost and forgotten all witting and feeling of his being, not looking after whether he have been holy or wretched. But whether this fall oft or seldom to a soul that is thus disposed, I trow that it lasteth but a full short while: and in this time it is perfectly meeked, for it knoweth and feeleth no cause but the Chief. And ever when it knoweth and feeleth the tother cause, communing therewith, although this be the chief: yet it is imperfect meekness. Nevertheless yet it is good and notwithstanding must be had; and God forbid that thou take it in any other manner than I say.

Here Beginneth
the Fourteenth Chapter

That without imperfect meekness coming before, it is impossible for a sinner to come to the perfect virtue of meekness in this life.

For although I call it imperfect meekness, yet I had liefer have a true knowing and a feeling of myself as I am, and sooner I trow that it should get me the perfect cause and virtue of meekness by itself, than it should an all the saints and angels in heaven, and all the men and women of Holy Church living in earth, religious or seculars in all degrees, were set at once all together to do nought else but to pray to God for me to get me perfect meekness. Yea, and yet it is impossible a sinner to get, or to keep when it is gotten, the perfect virtue of meekness without it.

And therefore swink and sweat in all that thou canst and mayest, for to get thee a true knowing and a feeling of thyself as thou art; and then I trow that soon after that thou shalt have a true knowing and a feeling of God as He is. Not as He is in Himself, for that may no man do but Himself; nor yet as thou shalt do in bliss both body and soul together. But as it is possible, and as He vouchsafeth to be known and felt of a meek soul living in this deadly body.

And think not because I set two causes of meekness, one perfect and another imperfect, that I will therefore that thou leavest the travail about imperfect meekness, and set thee wholly to get thee perfect. Nay, surely; I trow thou shouldest never bring it so about. But herefore I do that I do: because I think to tell thee and let thee see the worthiness of this ghostly exercise before all other exercise bodily or ghostly that man can or may do by grace. How that a privy love pressed in cleanness of spirit upon this dark cloud of unknowing betwixt thee and thy God, truly and perfectly containeth in it the perfect virtue of meekness without any special or clear beholding of any thing under God. And because I would that thou knewest which were perfect meekness, and settest it as a token before the love of thine heart, and didst it for thee and for me. And because I would by this knowing make thee more meek.

For ofttimes it befalleth that lacking of knowing is cause of much pride as me thinketh. For peradventure an thou knewest not which were perfect meekness, thou shouldest ween when thou hadst a little knowing and a feeling of this that I call imperfect meekness, that thou hadst almost gotten perfect meekness: and so shouldest thou deceive thyself, and ween that thou wert full meek when thou wert all belapped in foul stinking pride. And therefore try for to travail about perfect meekness; for the condition of it is such, that whoso hath it, and the whiles he hath it, he shall not sin, nor yet much after.

Here Beginneth the Fifteenth Chapter

A short proof against their error that say, that there is no per-fecter cause to be meeked under, than is the knowledge of a man's own wretchedness.

And trust steadfastly that there is such a perfect meekness as I speak of, and that it may be come to through grace in this life. And this I say in confusion of their error, that say that there is no perfecter cause of meekness than is that which is raised of the remembrance of our wretchedness and our before-done sins.

I grant well, that to them that have been in accustomed sins, as I am myself and have been, it is the most needful and speed-ful cause, to be meeked under the remembrance of our wretchedness and our before-done sins, ever till the time be that the great rust of sin be in great part rubbed away, our conscience and our counsel to witness. But to other that be, as it were, innocents, the which never sinned deadly with an abiding will and advisement, but through frailty and unknowing, and the which set them to be contemplatives—and to us both if our counsel and our conscience witness our lawful amendment in contrition and in confession, and in making satisfaction after the statute and the ordinance of all-Holy Church, and thereto if we feel us stirred and called by grace to be contemplatives also—there is then another cause to be meeked under as far above this cause as is the living of our Lady Saint Mary above the living of the sinfullest penitent in Holy Church; or the living of Christ above the living of any other man in this life; or else the living of an angel in heaven, the which never felt—nor shall feel—frailty, is above the life of the frailest man that is here in this world.

For if it so were that there were no perfect cause to be meeked under, but in seeing and feeling of wretchedness, then would I wit of them that say so, what cause they be meeked under that never see nor feel—nor never shall be in them—wretchedness nor stirring of sin: as it is of our Lord JESUS CHRIST, our Lady Saint Mary, and all the saints and angels in heaven. To this perfection, and all other, our Lord JESUS CHRIST calleth us Himself in the gospel: where He biddeth *that we should be perfect* by grace *as He Himself is* by nature.

Here Beginneth the Sixteenth Chapter

That by virtue of this work a sinner truly turned and called to contemplation cometh sooner to perfection than by any other work; and by it soonest may get of God forgiveness of sins.

Look that no man think it presumption, that he that is the wretchedest sinner of this life dare take upon him after the time be that he have lawfully amended him, and after that he have felt him stirred to that life that is called contemplative, by the assent of his counsel and his conscience for to profer a meek stirring of love to his God, privily pressing upon the cloud of unknowing betwixt him and his God. When our Lord said to Mary, in person of all sinners that be called to contemplative life, "Thy sins be forgiven thee," it was not for her great sorrow, nor for the remembering of her sins, nor yet for her meekness that she had in the beholding of her wretchedness only. But why then? Surely because she loved much.

Lo! here may men see what a privy pressing of love may purchase of our Lord, before all other works that man may think. And yet I grant well, that she had full much sorrow, and wept full sore for her sins, and full much she was meeked in remembrance of her wretchedness. And so should we do, that have been wretches and accustomed sinners; all our lifetime make hideous and wonderful sorrow for our sins, and full much be meeked in remembrance of our wretchedness.

But how? Surely as Mary did. She, although she might not feel the deep hearty sorrow of her sins—for why, all her lifetime she had them with her whereso she went, as it were in a burthen

bounden together and laid up full privily in the hole of her
heart, in manner never to be forgotten—nevertheless yet, it may
be said and affirmed by Scripture, that she had a more hearty
sorrow, a more doleful desire, and a more deep sighing, and
more she languished, yea! almost to the death, for lacking of
love, although she had full much love (and have no wonder
thereof, for it is the condition of a true lover that ever the more
he loveth, the more he longeth for to love), than she had for any
remembrance of her sins.

And yet she wist well, and felt well in herself in a sad soothfastness, that she was a wretch most foul of all other, and that
her sins had made a division betwixt her and her God that she
loved so much: and also that they were in great part cause of her
languishing sickness for lacking of love. But what thereof? Came
she therefore down from the height of desire into the deepness
of her sinful life, and searched in the foul stinking fen and
dunghill of her sins; searching them up, by one and by one, with
all the circumstances of them, and sorrowed and wept so upon
them each one by itself? Nay, surely she did not so. And why?
Because God let her wit by His grace within in her soul, that she
should never so bring it about. For so might she sooner have
raised in herself an ableness to have oft sinned, than to have
purchased by that work any plain forgiveness of all her sins.

And therefore she hung up her love and her longing desire in
this cloud of unknowing, and learned her to love a thing the
which she might not see clearly in this life, by light of understanding in her reason, nor yet verily feel in sweetness of love in
her affection. Insomuch, that she had ofttimes little special
remembrance, whether that ever she had been a sinner or none.
Yea, and full ofttimes I hope that she was so deeply disposed to
the love of His Godhead that she had but right little special
beholding unto the beauty of His precious and His blessed body,
in the which He sat full lovely speaking and preaching before
her; nor yet to anything else, bodily or ghostly. That this be
sooth, it seemeth by the gospel.

Here Beginneth
the Seventeenth Chapter

*That a very contemplative list not meddle him with active life,
nor of anything that is done or spoken about him, nor yet to
answer to his blamers in excusing of himself.*

In the gospel of Saint Luke it is written, that when our Lord
was in the house of Martha her sister, all the time that Martha
made her busy about the dighting of His meat, Mary her sister
sat at His feet. And in hearing of His word she beheld not to the
business of her sister, although her business was full good and
full holy, for truly it is the first part of active life; nor yet to the
preciousness of His blessed body, nor to the sweet voice and the
words of His manhood, although it is better and holier, for it is
the second part of active life and the first of contemplative life.

But to the sovereignest wisdom of His Godhead lapped in the
dark words of His manhood, thither beheld she with all the love
of her heart. For from thence she would not remove, for nothing that she saw nor heard spoken nor done about her; but sat
full still in her body, with many a sweet privy and a listy love
pressed upon that high cloud of unknowing betwixt her and her
God. For one thing I tell thee, that there was never yet pure
creature in this life, nor never yet shall be, so high ravished in
contemplation and love of the Godhead, that there is not evermore a high and a wonderful cloud of unknowing betwixt him
and his God. In this cloud it was that Mary was occupied with
many a privy love pressed. And why? Because it was the best
and the holiest part of contemplation that may be in this life,

and from this part her list not remove for nothing. Insomuch, that when her sister Martha complained to our Lord of her, and bade Him bid her sister rise and help her and let her not so work and travail by herself, she sat full still and answered not with one word, nor shewed not as much as a grumbling gesture against her sister for any plaint that she could make. And no wonder: for why, she had another work to do that Martha wist not of. And therefore she had no leisure to listen to her, nor to answer her at her plaint.

Lo! friend, all these works, these words, and these gestures, that were shewed betwixt our Lord and these two sisters, be set in ensample of all actives and all contemplatives that have been since in Holy Church, and shall be to the day of doom. For by Mary is understood all contemplatives; for they should conform their living after hers. And by Martha, actives on the same manner; and for the same reason in likeness.

Here Beginneth
the Eighteenth Chapter

How that yet unto this day all actives complain of contempla-
tives as Martha did of Mary. Of the which complaining igno-
rance is the cause.

And right as Martha complained then on Mary her sister,
right so yet unto this day all actives complain of contemplatives. For an there be a man or a woman in any company of
this world, what company soever it be, religious or seculars—I
out-take none—the which man or woman, whichever that it be,
feeleth him stirred through grace and by counsel to forsake all
outward business, and for to set him fully for to live contemplative life after their cunning and their conscience, their counsel
according; as fast, their own brethren and their sisters, and all
their next friends, with many other that know not their stirrings
nor that manner of living that they set them to, with a great
complaining spirit shall rise upon them, and say sharply unto
them that it is nought that they do. And as fast they will reckon
up many false tales, and many true also, of falling of men and
women that have given them to such life before: and never a
good tale of them that stood.

I grant that many fall and have fallen of them that have in likeness forsaken the world. And where they should have become
God's servants and His contemplatives, because that they would
not rule them by true ghostly counsel they have become the
devil's servants and his contemplatives; and turned either to hypocrites or to heretics, or fallen into frenzies and many other mischiefs, in slander of Holy Church. Of the which I leave to speak
at this time, for troubling of our matter. But nevertheless here-
after when God vouchsafeth and if need be, men may see some
of the conditions and the cause of their failings. And therefore no
more of them at this time; but forth of our matter.

Here Beginneth
the Nineteenth Chapter

A short excusation of him that made this book, teaching how all contemplatives should have all actives fully excused of their complaining words and deeds.

Some might think that I do little worship to Martha, that special saint, for I liken her words of complaining of her sister unto these worldly men's words, or theirs unto hers: and truly I mean no unworship to her nor to them. And God forbid that I should in this work say anything that might be taken in condemnation of any of the servants of God in any degree, and namely of His special saint. For me thinketh that she should be full well had excused of her plaint, taking regard to the time and the manner that she said it in. For that that she said, her unknowing was the cause. And no wonder though she knew not at that time how Mary was occupied; for I trow that before she had little heard of such perfection. And also that she said, it was but courteously and in few words: and therefore she should always be had excused.

And so me thinketh that these worldly living men and women of active life should also full well be had excused of their complaining words touched before, although they say rudely that they say; having beholding to their ignorance. For why? Right as Martha wist full little what Mary her sister did when she complained of her to our Lord; right so on the same manner these folk nowadays wot full little, or else nought, what these young disciples of God mean, when they set them from the business of

this world, and draw them to be God's special servants in holi-
ness and rightfulness of spirit. And if they wist truly, I daresay
that they would neither do nor say as they say. And therefore me
thinketh always that they should be had excused: for why, they
know no better living than is that they live in themselves. And
also when I think on mine innumerable defaults, the which I
have made myself before this time in words and deeds for
default of knowing, me thinketh then if I would be had excused
of God for mine ignorant defaults, that I should charitably and
piteously have other men's ignorant words and deeds always
excused. And surely else, do I not to others as I would they did
to me.

Here Beginneth
the Twentieth Chapter

How Almighty God will goodly answer for all those that for the excusing of themselves list not leave their business about the love of Him.

And therefore me thinketh, that they that set them to be contemplatives should not only have active men excused of their complaining words, but also me thinketh that they should be so occupied in spirit that they should take little heed or none what men did or said about them. Thus did Mary, our example of all, when Martha her sister complained to our Lord: and if we will truly do thus our Lord will do now for us as He did then for Mary.

And how was that? Surely thus. Our lovely Lord Jesus Christ, unto whom no privy thing is hid, although He was required of Martha as doomsman for to bid Mary rise and help her to serve Him; nevertheless yet, for He perceived that Mary was fervently occupied in spirit about the love of His Godhead, therefore courteously and as it was seemly for Him to do by the way of reason, He answered for her, that for the excusing of herself list not leave the love of Him. And how answered He? Surely not only as doomsman, as He was of Martha appealed: but as an advocate lawfully defended her that Him loved, and said, "Martha, Martha!" Twice for speed He named her name; for He would that she heard Him and took heed to His words. "Thou art full busy," He said, "and troubled about many things." For they that be actives behove always to be busied and travailed

THE TWENTIETH CHAPTER   41

about many diverse things, the which them falleth, first for to
have to their own use, and sithen in deeds of mercy to their
even-christian, as charity asketh. And this He said unto Martha,
for He would let her wit that her business was good and profitable to the health of her soul. But for this, that she should not
think that it were the best work of all that man might do, therefore He added and said: "But one thing is necessary."

And what is that one thing? Surely that God be loved and
praised by Himself, above all other business bodily or ghostly
that man may do. And for this, that Martha should not think that
she might both love God and praise Him above all other business bodily or ghostly, and also thereto to be busy about the necessaries of this life: therefore to deliver her of doubt that she
might not both serve God in bodily business and ghostly together perfectly—-imperfectly she may, but not perfectly—He
added and said, that Mary had chosen the best part; the which
should never be taken from her. For why, that perfect stirring of
love that beginneth here is even in number with that that shall
last without end in the bliss of heaven, for all it is but one.

Here Beginneth the One
and Twentieth Chapter

The true exposition of this gospel word,
"Mary hath chosen the best part."

What meaneth this; Mary hath chosen the best? Wheresoever the best is set or named, it asketh before it these two things—a good, and a better; so that it be the best, and the third in number. But which be these three good things, of the which Mary chose the best? Three lives be they not, for Holy Church maketh remembrance but of two, active life and contemplative life; the which two lives be privily understood in the story of this gospel by these two sisters Martha and Mary—by Martha active, by Mary contemplative. Without one of these two lives may no man be safe, and where no more be but two, may no man choose the best.

But although there be but two lives, nevertheless yet in these two lives be three parts, each one better than other. The which three, each one by itself, be specially set in their places before in this writing. For as it is said before, the first part standeth in good and honest bodily works of mercy and of charity; and this is the first degree of active life, as it is said before. The second part of these two lives lieth in good ghostly meditations of a man's own wretchedness, the Passion of Christ, and of the joys of heaven. The first part is good, and this part is the better; for this is the second degree of active life and the first of contemplative life. In this part is contemplative life and active life coupled together in ghostly kinship, and made sisters at the ensample of Martha and Mary. Thus high may an active come to contemplation; and no higher, but if it be full seldom and by a special grace. Thus low may a contemplative come towards active life; and no lower, but if it be full seldom and in great need.

The third part of these two lives hangeth in this dark cloud of unknowing, with many a privy love pressed to God by Himself. The first part is good, the second is better, but the third is best of all. This is the "best part" of Mary. And therefore it is plainly to wit, that our Lord said not, Mary hath chosen the best *life;* for there be no more lives but two, and of two may no man choose the best. But of these two lives Mary hath chosen, He said, the best *part;* the which shall never be taken from her. The first part and the second, although they be both good and holy, yet they end with this life. For in the tother life shall be no need as now to use the works of mercy, nor to weep for our wretchedness, nor for the Passion of Christ. For then shall none be able to hunger nor thirst as now, nor die for cold, nor be sick, nor houseless, nor in prison; nor yet need burial, for then shall none be able to die. But the third part that Mary chose, choose who by grace is called to choose: or, if I soothlier shall say, whoso is chosen thereto of God. Let him lustily incline thereto, for that shall never be taken away: for if it begin here, it shall last without end.

And therefore let the voice of our Lord cry on these actives, as if He said thus now for us unto them, as He did then for Mary to Martha, "Martha, Martha!"—"Actives, actives! make you as busy as ye can in the first part and in the second, now in the one and now in the tother: and, if you list right well and feel you disposed, in both two bodily. And meddle you not of contemplatives. Ye wot not what them aileth: let them sit in their rest and in their play, with the third and the best part of Mary."

Here Beginneth the Two and Twentieth Chapter

Of the wonderful love that Christ had to man in person of all sinners truly turned and called to the grace of contemplation.

Sweet was that love betwixt our Lord and Mary. Much love had she to Him. Much more had He to her. For whoso would utterly behold all the behaviour that was betwixt Him and her, not as a trifler may tell, but as the story of the gospel will witness—the which on nowise may be false—he should find that she was so heartily set for to love Him, that nothing beneath Him might comfort her, nor yet hold her heart from Him. This is she, that same Mary, that when she sought Him at the sepulchre with weeping cheer would not be comforted of angels. For when they spake unto her so sweetly and so lovely and said, "Weep not, Mary; for why, our Lord whom thou seekest is risen, and thou shalt have Him, and see Him live full fair amongst His disciples in Galilee as He hight," she would not cease for them. For why? Her thought that whoso sought verily the King of Angels, them list not cease for Angels.

And what more? Surely whoso will look verily in the story of the gospel, he shall find many wonderful points of perfect love written of her to our ensample, and as even according to the work of this writing, as if they had been set and written therefore; and surely so were they, take whoso take may. And if a man list for to see in the gospel written the wonderful and the special love that our Lord had to her, in person of all accustomed sinners truly turned and called to the grace of contemplation, he shall find that our Lord might not suffer any man or woman—yea, not her own sister—speak a word against her, but if He answered for her Himself. Yea, and what more? He blamed Symon Leprous in his own house, for that he thought against her. This was great love: this was passing love.

Here Beginneth the Three and Twentieth Chapter

How God will answer and purvey for them in spirit, that for business about His love list not answer nor purvey for themselves.

And truly an we will lustily conform our love and our living, inasmuch as in us is, by grace and by counsel, unto the love and the living of Mary, no doubt but He shall answer on the same manner now for us ghostly each day, privily in the hearts of all those that either say or think against us. I say not but that evermore some men shall say or think somewhat against us, the whiles we live in the travail of this life, as they did against Mary. But I say, an we will give no more heed to their saying nor to their thinking, nor no more cease of our ghostly privy work for their words and their thoughts, than she did—I say, then, that our Lord shall answer them in spirit, if it shall be well with them that so say and so think, that they shall within few days have shame of their words and their thoughts.

And as He will answer for us thus in spirit, so will He stir other men in spirit to give us our needful things that belong to this life, as meat and clothes with all these other; if He see that we will not leave the work of His love for business about them. And this I say in confusion of their error, that say that it is not lawful for men to set them to serve God in contemplative life, but if they be secure before of their bodily necessaries. For they say, that God sendeth the cow, but not by the horn. And truly they say wrong of God, as they well know. For trust steadfastly, thou whatsoever that thou be, that truly turnest thee from the world unto God, that one of these two God shall send thee, without business of thyself: and that is either abundance of necessaries, or strength in body and patience in spirit to bear need. What then recketh it, which man have? for all come to one in very contemplatives. And whoso is in doubt of this, either the devil is in his breast and reeveth him of belief, or else he is not yet truly turned to God as he should be; make he it never so quaint, nor never so holy reasons shew there again, whatsoever that he be.

And therefore thou, that settest thee to be contemplative as Mary was, choose thee rather to be meeked under the wonderful height and the worthiness of God, the which is perfect, than under thine own wretchedness, the which is imperfect: that is to say, look that thy special beholding be more to the worthiness of God than to thy wretchedness. For to them that be perfectly meeked, no thing shall defail; neither bodily thing, nor ghostly. For why? They have God, in whom is all plenty; and whoso hath Him—yea, as this book telleth—him needeth nought else in this life.

Here Beginneth the Four and Twentieth Chapter

What charity is in itself, and how it is truly and perfectly contained in the work of this book.

And as it is said of meekness, how that it is truly and perfectly comprehended in this little blind love pressed, when it is beating upon this dark cloud of unknowing, all other things put down and forgotten: so it is to be understood of all other virtues, and specially of charity.

For charity is nought else to bemean to thine understanding, but love of God for Himself above all creatures, and of man for God even as thyself. And that in this work God is loved for Himself, and above all creatures, it seemeth right well. For as it is said before, that the substance of this work is nought else but a naked intent directed unto God for Himself.

A naked intent I call it. For why, in this work a perfect prentice asketh neither releasing of pain, nor increasing of meed, nor shortly to say, nought but Himself. Insomuch, that neither he recketh nor looketh after whether that he be in pain or in bliss, else that His will be fulfilled that he loveth. And thus it seemeth that in this work God is perfectly loved for Himself, and that above all creatures. For in this work, a perfect worker may not suffer the memory of the holiest creature that ever God made to commune with him.

And that in this work the second and the lower branch of charity unto thine even-christian is verily and perfectly fulfilled, it seemeth by the proof. For why, in this work a perfect worker hath no special beholding unto any man by himself, whether that he be kin or stranger, friend or foe. For all men him thinks equally kin unto him, and no man stranger. All men him thinks be his friends, and none his foes. Insomuch, that him thinks all those that pain him and do him disease in this life, they be his full and his special friends: and him thinketh, that he is stirred to will them as much good, as he would to the homeliest friend that he hath.

Here Beginneth the Five and Twentieth Chapter

That in the time of this work a perfect soul hath no special beholding to any one man in this life.

I say not that in this work he shall have a special beholding to any man in this life, whether that he be friend or foe, kin or stranger; for that may not be if this work shall perfectly be done, as it is when all things under God be fully forgotten, as falleth for this work. But I say that he shall be made so virtuous and so charitable by the virtue of this work, that his will shall be afterwards, when he condescendeth to commune or to pray for his even-christian—not from all this work, for that may not be without great sin, but from the height of this work, the which is speedful and needful to do some time as charity asketh—as specially then directed to his foe as to his friend, his stranger as his kin. Yea, and some time more to his foe than to his friend.

Nevertheless, in this work he hath no leisure to look after who is his friend or his foe, his kin or his stranger. I say not but he shall feel some time—yea, full oft—his affection more homely to one, two, or three, than to all these other: for that is lawful to be, for many causes as charity asketh. For such an homely affection felt Christ to John and unto Mary, and unto Peter before many others. But I say, that in the time of this work shall all be equally homely unto him; for he shall feel then no cause, but only God. So that all shall be loved plainly and nakedly for God, and as well as himself.

For as all men were lost in Adam and all men that with work

49

will witness their will of salvation are saved or shall be by virtue of the Passion of only Christ: not in the same manner, but as it were in the same manner, a soul that is perfectly disposed to this work, and oned thus to God in spirit as the proof of this work witnesseth, doth that in it is to make all men as perfect in this work as itself is. For right as if a limb of our body feeleth sore, all the tother limbs be pained and diseased therefore, or if a limb fare well, all the remnant be gladded therewith—right so is it ghostly of all the limbs of Holy Church. For Christ is our head, and we be the limbs if we be in charity: and whoso will be a perfect disciple of our Lord's, him behoveth strain up his spirit in this work ghostly, for the salvation of all his brethren and sisters in nature, as our Lord did His body on the Cross. And how? Not only for His friends and His kin and His homely lovers, but generally for all mankind, without any special beholding more to one than to another. For all that will leave sin and ask mercy shall be saved through the virtue of His Passion. And as it is said of meekness and charity, so it is to be understood of all other virtues. For all they be truly comprehended in this little pressing of love, touched before.

Here Beginneth the Six and Twentieth Chapter

That without full special grace, or long use in common grace, the work of this book is right travailous; and in this work, which is the work of the soul helped by grace, and which is the work of only God.

And therefore travail fast awhile, and beat upon this high cloud of unknowing, and rest afterward. Nevertheless, a travail shall he have who so shall use him in this work; yea, surely! and that a full great travail, unless he have a more special grace, or else that he have of long time used him therein.

But I pray thee, wherein shall that travail be? Surely not in that devout stirring of love that is continually wrought in his will, not by himself, but by the hand of Almighty God: the which is evermore ready to work this work in each soul that is disposed thereto, and that doth that in him is, and hath done long time before, to enable him to this work.

But wherein then is this travail, I pray thee? Surely, this travail is all in treading down of the remembrance of all the creatures that ever God made, and in holding of them under the cloud of forgetting named before. In this is all the travail; for this is man's travail, with help of grace. And the tother above— that is to say, the stirring of love—that is the work of only God. And therefore do on thy work, and surely I promise thee He shall not fail in His.

Do on then fast; let see how thou bearest thee. Seest thou not how He standeth and abideth thee? For shame! Travail fast but awhile, and thou shalt soon be eased of the greatness and of the hardness of this travail. For although it be hard and strait in the beginning, when thou hast no devotion; nevertheless yet after, when thou hast devotion, it shall be made full restful and full light unto thee that before was full hard. And thou shalt have either little travail or none, for then will God work sometimes all by Himself. But not ever, nor yet no long time together, but when Him list and as Him list; and then wilt thou think it merry to let Him alone.

Then will He sometimes peradventure send out a beam of ghostly light, piercing this cloud of unknowing that is betwixt thee and Him; and shew thee some of His privity, the which man may not, nor cannot speak. Then shalt thou feel thine affection inflamed with the fire of His love, far more than I can tell thee, or may or will at this time. For of that work, that falleth to only God, dare I not take upon me to speak with my blabbering fleshly tongue: and shortly to say, although I durst I would do not. But of that work that falleth to man when he feeleth him stirred and helped by grace, list me well tell thee: for therein is the less peril of the two.

Here Beginneth the Seven and Twentieth Chapter

Who should work in the gracious work of this book.

First and foremost, I will tell thee who should work in this work, and when, and by what means: and what discretion thou shalt have in it. If thou asketh me who shall work thus, I answer thee—all that have forsaken the world in a true will, and thereto that give them not to active life, but to that life that is called contemplative life. All those should work in this grace and in this work, whatsoever that they be; whether they have been accustomed sinners or none.

Here Beginneth the Eight and Twentieth Chapter

That a man should not presume to work in this work before the time that he be lawfully cleansed in conscience of all his special deeds of sin.

But if thou asketh me when they should work in this work, then I answer thee and I say: that not ere they have cleansed their conscience of all their special deeds of sin done before, after the common ordinance of Holy Church.

For in this work, a soul drieth up in it all the root and the ground of sin that will always live in it after confession, be it never so busy. And, therefore, whoso will travail in this work, let him first cleanse his conscience; and afterward when he hath done that in him is lawfully, let him dispose him boldly but meekly thereto. And let him think, that he hath full long been holden therefrom. For this is that work in the which a soul should travail all his lifetime, though he had never sinned deadly. And the whiles that a soul is dwelling in this deadly flesh, it shall evermore see and feel this cumbrous cloud of unknowing betwixt him and God. And not only that, but in pain of the original sin it shall evermore see and feel that some of all the creatures that ever God made, or some of their works, will evermore press in remembrance betwixt it and God. And this is the right wisdom of God, that man, when he had sovereignty and lordship of all other creatures, because that he wilfully made him underling to the stirring of his subjects, leaving the bidding of God and his Maker; that right so after, when he would fulfil the bidding of God, he saw and felt all the creatures that should be beneath him, proudly press above him, betwixt him and his God.

Here Beginneth the Nine
and Twentieth Chapter

*That a man should bidingly travail in this work, and suffer the
pain thereof, and judge no man.*

And therefore, whoso coveteth to come to cleanness that he
lost for sin, and to win to that well-being where all woe
wanteth, him behoveth bidingly to travail in this work, and suffer the pain thereof, whatsoever that he be: whether he have
been an accustomed sinner or none.

All men have travail in this work; both sinners, and innocents
that never sinned greatly. But far greater travail have those that
have been sinners than they that have been none; and that is
great reason. Nevertheless, ofttimes it befalleth that some that
have been horrible and accustomed sinners come sooner to the
perfection of this work than those that have been none. And this
is the merciful miracle of our Lord, that so specially giveth His
grace, to the wondering of all this world. Now truly I hope that
on Doomsday it shall be fair, when that God shall be seen
clearly and all His gifts. Then shall some that now be despised
and set at little or nought as common sinners, and peradventure
some that now be horrible sinners, sit full seemly with saints in
His sight: when some of those that seem now full holy and be
worshipped of men as angels, and some of those yet peradventure, that never yet sinned deadly, shall sit full sorry amongst
hell caves.

Hereby mayest thou see that no man should be judged of
other here in this life, for good nor for evil that they do.
Nevertheless deeds may lawfully be judged, but not the man,
whether they be good or evil.

Here Beginneth the Thirtieth Chapter

Who should blame and condemn other men's defaults.

B ut I pray thee, of whom shall men's deeds be judged?
Surely of them that have power, and cure of their souls:
either given openly by the statute and the ordinance of Holy
Church, or else privily in spirit at the special stirring of the Holy
Ghost in perfect charity. Each man beware, that he presume not
to take upon him to blame and condemn other men's defaults,
but if he feel verily that he be stirred of the Holy Ghost within
in his work; for else may he full lightly err in his dooms. And
therefore beware: judge thyself as thee list betwixt thee and thy
God or thy ghostly father, and let other men alone.

Here Beginneth the One and Thirtieth Chapter

How a man should have him in beginning of this work against all thoughts and stirrings of sin.

And from the time that thou feelest that thou hast done that in thee is, lawfully to amend thee at the doom of Holy Church, then shalt thou set thee sharply to work in this work. And then if it so be that thy foredone special deeds will always press in thy remembrance betwixt thee and thy God, or any new thought or stirring of any sin either, thou shalt stalwartly step above them with a fervent stirring of love, and tread them down under thy feet. And try to cover them with a thick cloud of forgetting, as they never had been done in this life of thee nor of other man either. And if they oft rise, oft put them down: and shortly to say, as oft as they rise, as oft put them down. And if thee think that the travail be great, thou mayest seek arts and wiles and privy subtleties of ghostly devices to put them away: the which subtleties be better learned of God by the proof than of any man in this life.

Here Beginneth the Two
and Thirtieth Chapter

Of two ghostly devices that be helpful to a ghostly beginner in the work of this book.

Nevertheless, somewhat of this subtlety shall I tell thee as me think. Prove thou and do better, if thou better mayest. Do that in thee is, to let be as thou wist not that they press so fast upon thee betwixt thee and thy God. And try to look as it were over their shoulders, seeking another thing: the which thing is God, enclosed in a cloud of unknowing. And if thou do thus, I trow that within short time thou shalt be eased of thy travail. I trow that an this device be well and truly conceived, it is nought else but a longing desire unto God, to feel Him and see Him as it may be here: and such a desire is charity, and it obtaineth always to be eased.

Another device there is: prove thou if thou wilt. When thou feelest that thou mayest on nowise put them down, cower thou down under them as a caitiff and a coward overcome in battle, and think that it is but a folly to thee to strive any longer with them, and therefore thou yieldest thee to God in the hands of thine enemies. And feel then thyself as thou wert foredone for ever. Take good heed of this device I pray thee, for me think in the proof of this device thou shouldest melt all to water. And surely me think an this device be truly conceived it is nought else but a true knowing and a feeling of thyself as thou art, a wretch and a filthy, far worse than nought: the which knowing and feeling is meekness. And this meekness obtaineth to have God Himself mightily descending, to venge thee of thine enemies, for to take thee up, and cherishingly dry thine ghostly eyen; as the father doth the child that is in point to perish under the mouths of wild swine or wode biting bears.

Here Beginneth the Three and Thirtieth Chapter

That in this work a soul is cleansed both of his special sins and of the pain of them, and yet how there is no perfect rest in this life.

More devices tell I thee not at this time; for an thou have grace to feel the proof of these, I trow that thou shalt know better to learn me than I thee. For although it should be thus, truly yet me think that I am full far therefrom. And therefore I pray thee help me, and do thou for thee and for me.

Do on then, and travail fast awhile, I pray thee, and suffer meekly the pain if thou mayest not soon win to these arts. For truly it is thy purgatory, and then when thy pain is all passed and thy devices be given of God, and graciously gotten in custom; then it is no doubt to me that thou art cleansed not only of sin, but also of the pain of sin. I mean, of the pain of thy special foredone sins, and not of the pain of the original sin. For that pain shall always last on thee to thy death day, be thou never so busy. Nevertheless, it shall but little provoke thee, in comparison of this pain of thy special sins; and yet shalt thou not be without great travail. For out of this original sin will all day spring new and fresh stirrings of sin: the which thee behoveth all day to smite down, and be busy to shear away with a sharp double-edged dreadful sword of discretion. And hereby mayest thou see and learn, that there is no soothfast security, nor yet no true rest in this life.

Nevertheless, herefore shalt thou not go back, nor yet be overfeared of thy failing. For an it so be that thou mayest have grace to destroy the pain of thine foredone special deeds, in the manner before said—or better if thou better mayest—sure be thou, that the pain of the original sin, or else the new stirrings of sin that be to come, shall but right little be able to provoke thee.

Here Beginneth the Four
and Thirtieth Chapter

That God giveth this grace freely without any means, and that it may not be come to with means.

And if thou askest me by what means thou shalt come to this work, I beseech Almighty God of His great grace and His great courtesy to teach thee Himself. For truly I do thee well to wit that I cannot tell thee, and that is no wonder. For why, that is the work of only God, specially wrought in what soul that Him liketh without any desert of the same soul. For without it no saint nor no angel can think to desire it. And I trow that our Lord as specially and as oft—yea! and more specially and more oft—will vouchsafe to work this work in them that have been accustomed sinners, than in some other, that never grieved Him greatly in comparison of them. And this will He do, for He will be seen all-merciful and almighty; and for He will be seen to work as Him list, where Him list, and when Him list.

And yet He giveth not this grace, nor worketh not this work, in any soul that is unable thereto. And yet, there is no soul without this grace, able to have this grace: none, whether it be a sinner's soul or an innocent soul. For neither it is given for innocence, nor withholden for sin. Take good heed, that I say withholden, and not withdrawn. Beware of error here, I pray thee; for ever, the nearer men touch the truth, more wary men behoveth to be of error. I mean but well: if thou canst not conceive it, lay it by thy side till God come and teach thee. Do then so, and hurt thee not.

Beware of pride, for it blasphemeth God in His Gifts, and boldeneth sinners. Wert thou verily meek, thou shouldest feel of this work as I say: that God giveth it freely without any desert. The condition of this work is such, that the presence thereof enableth a soul for to have it and for to feel it. And that ableness may no soul have without it. The ableness to this work is oned to the work's self without departing; so that whoso feeleth this work is able thereto, and none else. Insomuch, that without this work a soul is as it were dead, and cannot covet it nor desire it. Forasmuch as thou willest it and desirest it, so much hast thou of it, and no more nor no less: and yet is it no will, nor no desire, but a thing thou wottest never what, that stirreth thee to will and desire thou wottest never what. Reck thee never if thou wittest no more, I pray thee: but do forth ever more and more, so that thou be ever doing.

And if I shall shortlier say, let that thing do with thee and lead thee whereso it list. Let it be the worker, and you but the sufferer: do but look upon it, and let it alone. Meddle thee not therewith as thou wouldest help it, for dread lest thou spill all. Be thou but the tree, and let it be the wright: be thou but the house, and let it be the husbandman dwelling therein. Be blind in this time, and shear away covetise of knowing, for it will more let thee than help thee. It sufficeth enough unto thee, that thou feelest thee stirred likingly with a thing thou wottest never what, else that in this stirring thou hast no special thought of any thing under God; and that thine intent be nakedly directed unto God.

And if it be thus, trust then steadfastly that it is only God that stirreth thy will and thy desire plainly by Himself, without means either on His part or on thine. And be not feared, for the devil may not come so near. He may never come to stir a man's will, but occasionally and by means from afar, be he never so subtle a devil. For sufficiently and without means may no good angel stir thy will: nor, shortly to say, nothing but only God. So that thou mayest conceive here by these words somewhat (but much more clearly by the proof), that in this work men shall use no means: nor yet men may not come thereto with means. All good means hang upon it, and it on no means; nor no means may lead thereto.

Here Beginneth the Five and Thirtieth Chapter

Of three means in the which a contemplative prentice should be occupied; in reading, thinking and praying.

Nevertheless, means there be in the which a contemplative prentice should be occupied, the which be these—Lesson, Meditation, and Orison: or else to thine understanding they may be called—Reading, Thinking, and Praying. Of these three thou shalt find written in another book of another man's work, much better than I can tell thee; and therefore it needeth not here to tell thee of the qualities of them. But this may I tell thee: these three be so coupled together, that unto them that be beginners and profiters—but not to them that be perfect, yea, as it may be here—thinking may not goodly be gotten, without reading or hearing coming before. All is one in manner, reading and hearing: clerks reading on books, and lewd men reading on clerks when they hear them preach the word of God. Nor prayer may not goodly be gotten in beginners and profiters, without thinking coming before.

See by the proof. In this same course, God's word either written or spoken is likened to a mirror. Ghostly, the eyes of thy soul is thy reason; thy conscience is thy visage ghostly. And right as thou seest that if a foul spot be in thy bodily visage, the eyes of the same visage may not see that spot nor wit where it is, without a mirror or a teaching of another than itself; right so it is ghostly, without reading or hearing of God's word it is impossible to man's understanding that a soul that is blinded in custom of sin should see the foul spot in his conscience.

And so following, when a man seeth in a bodily or ghostly mirror, or wots by other men's teaching, whereabouts the foul spot is on his visage, either bodily or ghostly; then at first, and not before, he runneth to the well to wash him. If this spot be any special sin, then is this well Holy Church, and this water confession, with the circumstances. If it be but a blind root and a stirring of sin, then is this well merciful God, and this water prayer, with the circumstances. And thus mayest thou see that no thinking may goodly be gotten in beginners and profiters, without reading or hearing coming before: nor praying without thinking.

Here Beginneth the Six
and Thirtieth Chapter

Of the meditations of them that continually travail in the work of this book.

But it is not so with them that continually work in the work of this book. For their meditations be but as they were sudden conceits and blind feelings of their own wretchedness, or of the goodness of God; without any means of reading or hearing coming before, and without any special beholding of any thing under God. These sudden conceits and these blind feelings be sooner learned of God than of man. I care not though thou haddest nowadays none other meditations of thine own wretchedness, nor of the goodness of God (I mean if thou feel thee thus stirred by grace and by counsel), but such as thou mayest have in this word SIN, and in this word GOD: or in such other, which as thee list. Not breaking nor expounding these words with curiosity of wit, in beholding after the qualities of these words, as thou wouldest by that beholding increase thy devotion. I trow it should never be so in this case and in this work. But hold them all whole these words; and mean by sin, a *lump,* thou wottest never what, none other thing but thyself. Me think that in this blind beholding of sin, thus congealed in a lump, none other thing than thyself, it should be no need to bind a madder thing, than thou shouldest be in this time. And yet peradventure, whoso looked upon thee should think thee full soberly disposed in thy body, without any changing of countenance; but sitting or going or lying, or leaning or standing or kneeling, whether thou wert, in a full sober restfulness.

Here Beginneth the Seven and Thirtieth Chapter

Of the special prayers of them that be continual workers in the work of this book.

And right as the meditations of them that continually work in this grace and in this work rise suddenly without any means, right so do their prayers. I mean of their special prayers, not of those prayers that be ordained of Holy Church. For they that be true workers in this work, they worship no prayer so much: and therefore they do them, in the form and in the statute that they be ordained of holy fathers before us. But their special prayers rise evermore suddenly unto God, without any means or any premeditation in special coming before, or going therewith.

And if they be in words, as they be but seldom, then be they but in full few words: yea, and in ever the fewer the better. Yea, and if it be but a little word of one syllable, me think it better than of two: and more, too, according to the work of the spirit, since it so is that a ghostly worker in this work should evermore be in the highest and the sovereignest point of the spirit. That this be sooth, see by ensample in the course of nature. A man or a woman, afraid with any sudden chance of fire or of man's death or what else that it be, suddenly in the height of his spirit, he is driven upon haste and upon need for to cry or for to pray after help. Yea, how? Surely, not in many words, nor yet in one word of two syllables. And why is that? For him thinketh it over long tarrying for to declare the need and the work of his spirit. And therefore he bursteth up hideously with a great spirit, and cryeth a little word, but of one syllable: as is this word "fire," or this word "out!"

And right as this little word "fire" stirreth rather and pierceth more hastily the ears of the hearers, so doth a little word of one syllable when it is not only spoken or thought, but privily meant in the deepness of spirit; the which is the height, for in ghostliness all is one, height and deepness, length and breadth. And rather it pierceth the ears of Almighty God than doth any long psalter unmindfully mumbled in the teeth. And herefore it is written, that short prayer pierceth heaven.

Here Beginneth the Eight and Thirtieth Chapter

How and why that short prayer pierceth heaven.

And why pierceth it heaven, this little short prayer of one little syllable? Surely because it is prayed with a full spirit, in the height and in the deepness, in the length and in the breadth of his spirit that prayeth it. In the height it is, for it is with all the might of the spirit. In the deepness it is, for in this little syllable be contained all the wits of the spirit. In the length it is, for might it ever feel as it feeleth, ever would it cry as it cryeth. In the breadth it is, for it willeth the same to all other that it willeth to itself.

In this time it is that a soul hath comprehended after the lesson of Saint Paul with all saints—not fully, but in manner and in part, as it is according unto this work—which is the length and the breadth, the height and the deepness of everlasting and all-lovely, almighty, and all-witting God. The everlastingness of God is His length. His love is His breadth. His might is His height. And His wisdom is His deepness. No wonder though a soul that is thus nigh conformed by grace to the image and the likeness of God his maker, be soon heard of God! Yea, though it be a full sinful soul, the which is to God as it were an enemy; an he might through grace come for to cry such a little syllable in the height and the deepness, the length and the breadth of his spirit, yet he should for the hideous noise of his cry be always heard and helped of God.

See by ensample. He that is thy deadly enemy, an thou hear

67

him so afraid that he cry in the height of his spirit this little word "fire," or this word "out"; yet without any beholding to him for he is thine enemy, but for pure pity in thine heart stirred and raised with the dolefulness of this cry, thou risest up—yea, though it be about midwinter's night—and helpest him to slack his fire, or for to still him and rest him in his distress. Oh, Lord! since a man may be made so merciful in grace, to have so much mercy and so much pity of his enemy, notwithstanding his enmity, what pity and what mercy shall God have then of a ghostly cry in soul, made and wrought in the height and the deepness, the length and the breadth of his spirit; the which hath all by nature that man hath by grace? And much more, surely without comparison, much more mercy will He have; since it is, that that thing that is so had by nature is nearer to an eternal thing than that which is had by grace.

Here Beginneth the Nine and Thirtieth Chapter

How a perfect worker shall pray, and what prayer is in itself; and if a man shall pray in words, which words accord them most to the property of prayer.

And therefore it is, to pray in the height and the deepness, the length and the breadth of our spirit. And that not in many words, but in a little word of one syllable.

And what shall this word be? Surely such a word as is best according unto the property of prayer. And what word is that? Let us first see what prayer is properly in itself, and thereafter we may clearlier know what word will best accord to the property of prayer.

Prayer in itself properly is not else, but a devout intent direct unto God, for getting of good and removing of evil. And then, since it so is that all evil be comprehended in sin, either by cause or by being, let us therefore when we will intentively pray for removing of evil either say, or think, or mean, nought else nor no more words, but this little word "sin." And if we will intentively pray for getting of good, let us cry, either with word or with thought or with desire, nought else nor no more words, but this word "God." For why, in God be all good, both by cause and by being. Have no marvel why I set these words forby all other. For if I could find any shorter words, so fully comprehending in them all good and all evil, as these two words do, or if I had been learned of God to take any other words either, I would then have taken them and left these; and so I counsel that thou do.

69

Study thou not for no words, for so shouldest thou never come to thy purpose nor to this work, for it is never got by study, but all only by grace. And therefore take thou none other words to pray in, although I set these here, but such as thou art stirred of God for to take. Nevertheless, if God stir thee to take these, I counsel not that thou leave them; I mean if thou shalt pray in words, and else not. For why, they be full short words. But although the shortness of prayer be greatly commended here, nevertheless the oftness of prayer is never the rather refrained. For as it is said before, it is prayed in the length of the spirit; so that it should never cease, till the time were that it had fully gotten that that it longed after. Ensample of this have we in a man or a woman afraid in the manner beforesaid. For we see well, that they cease never crying on this little word "out," or this little word "fire," ere the time be that they have in great part gotten help of their grief.

Here Beginneth the Fortieth Chapter

That in the time of this work a soul hath no special beholding to any vice in itself nor to any virtue in itself.

D o thou, on the same manner, fill thy spirit with the ghostly bemeaning of this word "sin," and without any special beholding unto any kind of sin, whether it be venial or deadly: Pride, Wrath, or Envy, Covetyse, Sloth, Gluttony, or Lechery. What recks it in contemplatives, what sin that it be, or how muckle a sin that it be? For all sins them thinketh—I mean for the time of this work—alike great in themselves, when the least sin departeth them from God, and letteth them of their ghostly peace.

And feel sin a lump, thou wottest never what, but none other thing than thyself. And cry then ghostly ever upon one: *"Sin, sin, sin! Out, out, out!"* This ghostly cry is better learned of God by the proof, than of any man by word. For it is best when it is in pure spirit, without special thought or any pronouncing of word; unless it be any seldom time, when for abundance of spirit it bursteth up into word, so that the body and the soul be both filled with sorrow and cumbering of sin.

On the same manner shalt thou do with this little word "God." Fill thy spirit with the ghostly bemeaning of it without any special beholding to any of His works—whether they be good, better, or best of all—bodily or ghostly, or to any virtue that may be wrought in man's soul by any grace; not looking after whether it be meekness or charity, patience or abstinence, hope, faith, or soberness, chastity or wilful poverty. What recks this in contemplatives? For all virtues they find and feel in God; for in Him is all thing, both by cause and by being. For they think that an they had God they had all good, and therefore they covet nothing with special beholding, but only good God. Do thou on the same manner as far forth as thou mayest by grace: and mean God all, and all God, so that nought work in thy wit and in thy will, but only God.

And because that ever the whiles thou livest in this wretched life, thee behoveth always feel in some part this foul stinking lump of sin, as it were oned and congealed with the substance of thy being, therefore shalt thou changeably mean these two words—sin and God. With this general knowing, that an thou haddest God, then shouldest thou lack sin: and mightest thou lack sin, then shouldest thou have God.

Here Beginneth the One and Fortieth Chapter

That in all other works beneath this, men should keep discretion; but in this none.

And furthermore, if thou ask me what discretion thou shalt have in this work, then I answer thee and say, right none! For in all thine other doings thou shalt have discretion, as in eating and in drinking, and in sleeping and in keeping of thy body from outrageous cold or heat, and in long praying or reading, or in communing in speech with thine even-christian. In all these shalt thou keep discretion, that they be neither too much nor too little. But in this work shalt thou hold no measure: for I would that thou shouldest never cease of this work the whiles thou livest.

I say not that thou shalt continue ever therein alike fresh, for that may not be. For sometime sickness and other unordained dispositions in body and in soul, with many other needfulness to nature, will let thee full much, and ofttimes draw thee down from the height of this working. But I say that thou shouldest evermore have it either in earnest or in game; that is to say, either in work or in will. And therefore for God's love be wary with sickness as much as thou mayest goodly, so that thou be not the cause of thy feebleness, as far as thou mayest. For I tell thee truly, that this work asketh a full great restfulness, and a full whole and clean disposition, as well in body as in soul.

And therefore for God's love govern thee discreetly in body and in soul, and get thee thine health as much as thou mayest. And if sickness come against thy power, have patience and abide meekly God's mercy: and all is then good enough. For I tell thee truly, that ofttimes patience in sickness and in other diverse tribulations pleaseth God much more than any liking devotion that thou mayest have in thy health.

Here Beginneth the Two and Fortieth Chapter

That by indiscretion in this, men shall keep discretion in all other things; and surely else never.

But peradventure thou askest me, how thou shalt govern thee discreetly in meat and in sleep, and in all these other. And hereto I think to answer thee right shortly: "Get that thou get mayest." Do this work evermore without ceasing and without discretion, and thou shalt well ken begin and cease in all other works with a great discretion. For I may not trow that a soul continuing in this work night and day without discretion, should err in any of these outward doings; and else, me think that he should always err.

And therefore, an I might get a waking and a busy beholding to this ghostly work within in my soul, I would then have a heedlessness in eating and in drinking, in sleeping and in speaking, and in all mine outward doings. For surely I trow I should rather come to discretion in them by such a heedlessness, than by any busy beholding to the same things, as I would by that beholding set a mark and a measure by them. Truly I should never bring it so about, for ought that I could do or say. Say what men say will, and let the proof witness. And therefore lift up thine heart with a blind stirring of love; and mean now sin, and now God. God wouldest thou have, and sin wouldest thou lack. God wanteth thee; and sin art thou sure of. Now good God help thee, for now hast thou need!

Here Beginneth the Three and Fortieth Chapter

That all witting and feeling of a man's own being must needs be lost if the perfection of this work shall verily be felt in any soul in this life.

Look that nought work in thy wit nor in thy will but only God. And try for to fell all witting and feeling of ought under God, and tread all down full far under the cloud of forgetting. And thou shalt understand, that thou shalt not only in this work forget all other creatures than thyself, or their deeds or thine, but also thou shalt in this work forget both thyself and also thy deeds for God, as well as all other creatures and their deeds. For it is the condition of a perfect lover, not only to love that thing that he loveth more than himself; but also in a manner for to hate himself for that thing that he loveth.

Thus shalt thou do with thyself: thou shalt loathe and be weary with all that thing that worketh in thy wit and in thy will unless it be only God. For why, surely else, whatsoever that it be, it is betwixt thee and thy God. And no wonder though thou loathe and hate for to think on thyself, when thou shalt always feel sin, a foul stinking lump thou wottest never what, betwixt thee and thy God: the which lump is none other thing than thyself. For thou shalt think it oned and congealed with the substance of thy being: yea, as it were without departing.

And therefore break down all witting and feeling of all manner of creatures; but most busily of thyself. For on the witting and the feeling of thyself hangeth witting and feeling of all other

creatures; for in regard of it, all other creatures be lightly forgotten. For, an thou wilt busily set thee to the proof, thou shalt
find when thou hast forgotten all other creatures and all their
works—yea, and thereto all thine own works—that there shall
live yet after, betwixt thee and thy God, a naked witting and a
feeling of thine own being: the which witting and feeling
behoveth always be destroyed, ere the time be that thou feel
soothfastly the perfection of this work.

Here Beginneth the Four
and Fortieth Chapter

How a soul shall dispose it on its own part, for to destroy all wit-
ting and feeling of its own being.

But now thou askest me, how thou mayest destroy this naked
witting and feeling of thine own being. For peradventure
thou thinkest that an it were destroyed, all other lettings were
destroyed: and if thou thinkest thus, thou thinkest right truly.
But to this I answer thee and I say, that without a full special
grace full freely given of God, and thereto a full according ableness to receive this grace on thy part, this naked witting and
feeling of thy being may on nowise be destroyed. And this ableness is nought else but a strong and a deep ghostly sorrow.

But in this sorrow needeth thee to have discretion, on this
manner: thou shalt be wary in the time of this sorrow, that thou
neither too rudely strain thy body nor thy spirit, but sit full still,
as it were in a sleeping device, all forsobbed and forsunken in
sorrow. This is true sorrow; this is perfect sorrow; and well were
him that might win to this sorrow. All men have matter of sorrow: but most specially he feeleth matter of sorrow, that wotteth
and feeleth that he is. All other sorrows be unto this in comparison but as it were game to earnest. For he may make sorrow
earnestly, that wotteth and feeleth not only what he is, but that
he is. And whoso felt never this sorrow, he may make sorrow: for
why, he felt yet never perfect sorrow. This sorrow, when it is
had, cleanseth the soul, not only of sin, but also of pain that it
hath deserved for sin; and thereto it maketh a soul able to

receive that joy, the which reeveth from a man all witting and feeling of his being.

This sorrow, if it be truly conceived, is full of holy desire: and else might never man in this life abide it nor bear it. For were it not that a soul were somewhat fed with a manner of comfort of his right working, else should he not be able to bear the pain that he hath of the witting and feeling of his being. For as oft as he would have a true witting and a feeling of his God in purity of spirit, as it may be here, and sithen feeleth that he may not—for he findeth evermore his witting and his feeling as it were occupied and filled with a foul stinking lump of himself, the which behoveth always be hated and be despised and forsaken, if he shall be God's perfect disciple learned of Himself in the mount of perfection—so oft, he goeth nigh mad for sorrow. Insomuch, that he weepeth and waileth, striveth, curseth, and banneth; and shortly to say, him thinketh that he beareth so heavy a burthen of himself that he careth never what betides him, so that God were pleased. And yet in all this sorrow he desireth not to unbe: for that were devil's madness and despite unto God. But him listeth right well to be; and he intendeth full heartily thanking to God, for the worthiness and the gift of his being, for all that he desire unceasingly for to lack the witting and the feeling of his being.

This sorrow and this desire behoveth every soul have and feel in itself, either in this manner or in another; as God vouchsafeth for to learn to His ghostly disciples after His well willing and their according ableness in body and in soul, in degree and disposition, ere the time be that they may perfectly be oned unto God in perfect charity—such as may be had here—if God vouchsafeth.

Here Beginneth the Five
and Fortieth Chapter

A good declaring of some certain deceits that may befall in this work.

But one thing I tell thee, that in this work may a young disciple that hath not yet been well used and proved in ghostly working, full lightly be deceived; and, but he be soon wary, and have grace to leave off and meek him to counsel, peradventure be destroyed in his bodily powers and fall into fantasy in his ghostly wits. And all this is along of pride, and of fleshliness and curiosity of wit.

And on this manner may this deceit befall. A young man or a woman new set to the school of devotion heareth this sorrow and this desire be read and spoken: how that a man shall lift up his heart unto God, and unceasingly desire for to feel the love of his God. And as fast in a curiosity of wit they conceive these words not ghostly as they be meant, but fleshly and bodily; and travail their fleshly hearts outrageously in their breasts. And what for lacking of grace and pride and curiosity in themselves, they strain their veins and their bodily powers so beastly and so rudely, that within short time they fall either into frenzies, weariness, and a manner of unlisty feebleness in body and in soul, the which maketh them to wend out of themselves and seek some false and some vain fleshly and bodily comfort without, as it were for recreation of body and of spirit: or else, if they fall not in this, else they merit for ghostly blindness, and for fleshly chafing of their nature in their bodily breasts in the time of this feigned beastly and not ghostly working, for to have their breasts either enflamed with an unkindly heat of nature caused of misruling of their bodies or of this feigned working, or else they conceive a false heat wrought by the Fiend, their ghostly enemy, caused of their pride and of their fleshliness and their curiosity of wit. And yet peradventure they ween it be the fire of love, gotten and kindled by the grace and the goodness of the Holy Ghost. Truly, of this deceit, and of the branches thereof, spring many mischiefs: much hypocrisy, much heresy, and much error. For as fast after such a false feeling cometh a false knowing in the Fiend's school, right as after a true feeling cometh a true knowing in God's school. For I tell thee truly, that the devil hath his contemplatives as God hath His.

This deceit of false feeling, and of false knowing following thereon, hath diverse and wonderful variations, after the diversity of states and the subtle conditions of them that be deceived: as hath the true feeling and knowing of them that be saved. But I set no more deceits here but those with the which I trow thou shalt be assailed if ever thou purpose thee to work in this work. For what should it profit to thee to wit how these great clerks, and men and women of other degrees than thou art, be deceived? Surely right nought; and therefore I tell thee no more but those that fall unto thee if thou travail in this work. And therefore I tell thee this, for thou shalt be wary therewith in thy working, if thou be assailed therewith.

Here Beginneth the Six and Fortieth Chapter

A good teaching how a man shall flee these deceits, and work more with a listiness of spirit, than with any boisterousness of body.

And therefore for God's love be wary in this work, and strain not thine heart in thy breast over-rudely nor out of measure; but work more with a list than with any worthless strength. For ever the more listily, the more meekly and ghostly: and ever the more rudely, the more bodily and beastly. And therefore be wary, for surely what beastly heart that presumeth for to touch the high mount of this work, it shall be beaten away with stones. Stones be hard and dry in their kind, and they hurt full sore where they hit. And surely such rude strainings be full hard fastened in fleshliness of bodily feeling, and full dry from any witting of grace; and they hurt full sore the silly soul, and make it fester in fantasy feigned of fiends. And therefore be wary with this beastly rudeness, and learn thee to love listily, with a soft and a demure behaviour as well in body as in soul; and abide courteously and meekly the will of our Lord, and snatch not overhastily, as it were a greedy greyhound, hunger thee never so sore. And, gamingly be it said, I counsel that thou do that in thee is, refraining the rude and the great stirring of thy spirit, right as thou on nowise wouldest let Him wit how fain thou wouldest see Him, and have Him or feel Him.

This is childishly and playingly spoken, thee think peradventure. But I trow whoso had grace to do and feel as I say, he should feel good gamesome play with Him, as the father doth with the child, kissing and clipping, that well were him so.

Here Beginneth the Seven
and Fortieth Chapter

A slight teaching of this work in purity of spirit; declaring how that on one manner a soul should shew his desire unto God, and on ye contrary unto man.

L ook thou have no wonder why that I speak thus childishly, and as it were follily and lacking natural discretion; for I do it for certain reasons, and as me thinketh that I have been stirred many days, both to feel thus and think thus and say thus, as well to some other of my special friends in God, as I am now unto thee.

And one reason is this, why that I bid thee hide from God the desire of thine heart. For I hope it should more clearly come to His knowing, for thy profit and in fulfilling of thy desire, by such an hiding, than it should by any other manner of shewing that I trow thou couldest yet shew. And another reason is, for I would by such a hid shewing bring thee out of the boisterousness of bodily feeling into the purity and deepness of ghostly feeling; and so furthermore at the last to help thee to knit the ghostly knot of burning love betwixt thee and thy God, in ghostly one-head and according of will.

Thou wottest well this, that God is a Spirit; and whoso should be oned unto Him, it behoveth to be in soothfastness and deepness of spirit, full far from any feigned bodily thing. Sooth it is that all thing is known of God, and nothing may be hid from His witting, neither bodily thing nor ghostly. But more openly is that thing known and shewed unto Him, the which is hid in

82

deepness of spirit, sith it so is that He is a Spirit, than is anything that is mingled with any manner of bodilyness. For all bodily thing is farther from God by the course of nature than any ghostly thing. By this reason it seemeth, that the whiles our desire is mingled with any matter of bodilyness, as it is when we stress and strain us in spirit and in body together, so long it is farther from God than it should be, an it were done more devoutly and more listily in soberness and in purity and in deepness of spirit.

And here mayest thou see somewhat and in part the reason why that I bid thee so childishly cover and hide the stirring of thy desire from God. And yet I bid thee not plainly hide it; for that were the bidding of a fool, for to bid thee plainly do that which on nowise may be done. But I bid thee do that in thee is to hide it. And why bid I thus? Surely because I would that thou cast it into deepness of spirit, far from any rude mingling of any bodilyness, the which would make it less ghostly and farther from God inasmuch: and because I wot well that ever the more that thy spirit hath of ghostliness, the less it hath of bodilyness and the nearer it is to God, and the better it pleaseth Him and the more clearly it may be seen of Him. Not that His sight may be any time or in any thing more clear than in another, for it is evermore unchangeable: but because it is more like unto Him, when it is in purity of spirit, for He is a Spirit.

Another reason there is, why that I bid thee do that in thee is to let Him not wit: for thou and I and many such as we be, we be so able to conceive a thing bodily the which is said ghostly, that peradventure an I had bidden thee shew unto God the stirring of thine heart, thou shouldest have made a bodily shewing unto Him, either in gesture or in voice, or in word, or in some other rude bodily straining, as it is when thou shalt shew a thing that is hid in thine heart to a bodily man: and insomuch thy work should have been impure. For on one manner shall a thing be shewed to man, and on another manner unto God.

Here Beginneth the Eight
and Fortieth Chapter

How God will be served both with body and with soul, and reward men in both; and how men shall know when all those sounds and sweetness that fall into the body in time of prayer be both good and evil.

I say not this because I will that thou desist any time, if thou be stirred for to pray with thy mouth, or for to burst out for abundance of devotion in thy spirit for to speak unto God as unto man, and say some good word as thou feelest thee stirred: as be these, "Good JESU! Fair JESU! Sweet JESU!" and all such other! Nay, God forbid thou take it thus! For truly I mean not thus, and God forbid that I should depart that which God hath coupled, the body and the spirit. For God will be served with body and with soul both together, as seemly is, and will reward man his meed in bliss, both in body and in soul. And in earnest of that meed, sometimes He will enflame the body of devout servants of His here in this life: not once or twice, but peradventure right oft and as Him liketh, with full wonderful sweetness and comforts. Of the which, some be not coming from without into the body by the windows of our wits, but from within; rising and springing of abundance of ghostly gladness, and of true devotion in the spirit. Such a comfort and such a sweetness shall not be had suspect: and shortly to say, I trow that he that feeleth it may not have it suspect.

But all other comforts, sounds and gladness and sweetness, that come from without suddenly and thou wottest never whence, I pray thee have them suspect. For they may be both good and evil; wrought by a good angel if they be good, and by an evil angel if they be evil. And this may on nowise be evil, if their deceits of curiosity of wit, and of unordained straining of the fleshly heart be removed as I learn thee, or better if thou better mayest. And why is that? Surely for the cause of this comfort; that is to say, the devout stirring of love, the which dwelleth in pure spirit. It is wrought of the hand of Almighty God without means, and therefore it behoveth always be far from any fantasy, or any false opinion that may befall to man in this life.

And of the tother comforts and sounds and sweetness, how thou shouldest wit whether they be good or evil I think not to tell thee at this time: and that is because me think that it needeth not. For why, thou mayest find it written in another place of another man's work, a thousandfold better than I can say or write: and so mayest thou this that I set here, far better than it is here. But what thereof? Therefore shall I not let, nor it shall not noye me, to fulfil the desire and the stirring of thine heart; the which thou hast shewed thee to have unto me before this time in thy words, and now in thy deeds.

But this may I say thee of those sounds and of those sweetnesses, that come in by the windows of thy wits, the which may be both good and evil. Use thee continually in this blind and devout and this listy stirring of love that I tell thee: and then I have no doubt, that it shall not well be able to tell thee of them. And if thou yet be in part astonished of them at the first time, and that is because that they be uncouth, yet this shall it do thee: it shall bind thine heart so fast, that thou shalt on nowise give full great credence to them, ere the time be that thou be either certified of them within wonderfully by the Spirit of God, or else without by counsel of some discreet father.

Here Beginneth the Nine
and Fortieth Chapter

The substance of all perfection is nought else but a good will; and how that all sounds and comfort and sweetness that may befall in this life be to it but as it were accidents.

And therefore I pray thee, lean listily to this meek stirring of love in thine heart, and follow thereafter: for it will be thy guide in this life and bring thee to bliss in the tother. It is the substance of all good living, and without it no good work may be begun nor ended. It is nought else but a good and an according will unto God, and a manner of well-pleasedness and a gladness that thou feelest in thy will of all that He doth.

Such a good will is the substance of all perfection. All sweetness and comforts, bodily or ghostly, be to this but as it were accidents, be they never so holy; and they do but hang on this good will. Accidents I call them, for they may be had and lacked without breaking asunder of it. I mean in this life, but it is not so in the bliss of heaven; for there shall they be oned with the substance without departing, as shall the body in the which they work with the soul. So that the substance of them here is but a good ghostly will. And surely I trow that he that feeleth the perfection of this will, as it may be had here, there may no sweetness nor no comfort fall to any man in this life, that he is not as fain and as glad to lack it at God's will, as to feel it and have it.

Here Beginneth the Fiftieth Chapter

Which is chaste love; and how in some creatures such sensible comforts be but seldom, and in some right oft.

And hereby mayest thou see that we should direct all our beholding unto this meek stirring of love in our will. And in all other sweetness and comforts, bodily or ghostly, be they never so liking nor so holy, if it be courteous and seemly to say, we should have a manner of recklessness. If they come, welcome them: but lean not too much on them for fear of feebleness, for it will take full much of thy powers to bide any long time in such sweet feelings and weepings. And peradventure thou mayest be stirred for to love God for them, and that shalt thou feel by this: if thou grumble overmuch when they be away. And if it be thus, thy love is not yet neither chaste nor perfect. For a love that is chaste and perfect, though it suffer that the body be fed and comforted in the presence of such sweet feelings and weepings, nevertheless yet it is not grumbling, but full well pleased for to lack them at God's will. And yet it is not commonly without such comforts in some creatures, and in some other creatures such sweetness and comforts be but seldom.

And all this is after the disposition and the ordinance of God, all after the profit and the needfulness of diverse creatures. For some creatures be so weak and so tender in spirit, that unless they were somewhat comforted by feeling of such sweetness, they might on nowise abide nor bear the diversity of temptations and tribulations that they suffer and be travailed with in this life of their bodily and ghostly enemies. And some there be that they be so weak in body that they may do no great penance to cleanse them with. And these creatures will our Lord cleanse full graciously in spirit by such sweet feelings and weepings. And also on the tother part there be some creatures so strong in spirit, that they can pick them comfort enough within in their souls, in offering up of this reverent and this meek stirring of love and accordance of will, that them needeth not much to be fed with such sweet comforts in bodily feelings. Which of these be holier or more dear with God, one than another, God wots and I not.

Here Beginneth the One and Fiftieth Chapter

That men should have great wariness so that they understand not bodily a thing that is meant ghostly; and specially it is good to be wary in understanding of this word "in," and of this word "up."

And therefore lean meekly to this blind stirring of love in thine heart. I mean not in thy bodily heart, but in thy ghostly heart, the which is thy will. And be well wary that thou conceive not bodily that that is said ghostly. For truly I tell thee, that bodily and fleshly conceits of them that have curious and imaginative wits be cause of much error.

Ensample of this mayest thou see, by that that I bid thee hide thy desire from God in that that in thee is. For peradventure an I had bidden thee shew thy desire unto God, thou shouldest have conceived it more bodily than thou dost now, when I bid thee hide it. For thou wottest well, that all that thing that is wilfully hidden, it is cast into the deepness of spirit. And thus me thinketh that it needeth greatly to have much wariness in understanding of words that be spoken to ghostly intent, so that thou conceive them not bodily but ghostly, as they be meant: and specially it is good to be wary with this word *in,* and this word *up.* For in misconceiving of these two words hangeth much error, and much deceit in them that purpose them to be ghostly workers, as me thinketh. Somewhat wot I by the proof, and somewhat by hearsay; and of these deceits list me tell thee a little as me thinketh.

A young disciple in God's school new turned from the world, the same weeneth that for a little time that he hath given him to penance and to prayer, taken by counsel in confession, that he be therefore able to take upon him ghostly working of the which he heareth men speak or read about him, or peradventure readeth himself. And therefore when they read or hear spoken of ghostly working—and specially of this word, "how a man shall draw all his wit within himself," or "how he shall climb above himself"—as fast for blindness in soul, and for fleshliness and curiosity of natural wit, they misunderstand these words, and ween, because they find in them a natural covetyse to hid things, that they be therefore called to that work by grace. Insomuch, that if counsel will not accord that they shall work in this work, as soon they feel a manner of grumbling against their counsel, and think—yea and peradventure say to such other as they be— that they can find no man that can wit what they mean fully. And therefore as fast, for boldness and presumption of their curious wit, they leave meek prayer and penance over soon; and set them, they ween, to a full ghostly work within in their soul. The which work, an it be truly conceived, is neither bodily working nor ghostly working; and shortly to say, it is a working against nature, and the devil is the chief worker thereof. And it is the readiest way to death of body and of soul, for it is madness and no wisdom, and leadeth a man even to madness. And yet they ween not thus: for they purpose them in this work to think on nought but on God.

Here Beginneth the Two and Fiftieth Chapter

How these young presumptuous disciples misunderstand this word "in," and of the deceits that follow thereon.

And on this manner is this madness wrought that I speak of. They read and hear well said that they should leave outward working with their wits, and work inwards: and because that they know not which is inward working, therefore they work wrong. For they turn their bodily wits inwards to their body against the course of nature; and strain them, as they would see inwards with their bodily eyes and hear inwards with their ears, and so forth of all their wits, smelling, tasting, and feeling inwards. And thus they reverse them against the course of nature, and with this curiosity they travail their imagination so indiscreetly, that at the last they turn their brain in their heads, and then as fast the devil hath power for to feign some false light or sounds, sweet smells in their noses, wonderful tastes in their mouths; and many quaint heats and burnings in their bodily breasts or in their bowels, in their backs and in their reins and in their members.

And yet in this fantasy them think that they have a restful remembrance of their God without any letting of vain thoughts; and surely so have they in manner, for they be so filled in false-hood that vanity may not provoke them. And why? Because he, that same fiend that should minister vain thoughts to them an they were in good way—he, that same, is the chief worker of this work. And wit thou right well, that him list not to let himself. The remembrance of God will he not put from them, for fear that he should be had in suspect.

Here Beginneth the Three and Fiftieth Chapter

Of divers unseemly practices that follow them that lack the work of this book.

Many wonderful practices follow them that be deceived in this false work, or in any species thereof, beyond that doth them that be God's true disciples: for they be evermore full seemly in all their practices, bodily or ghostly. But it is not so of these other. For whoso would or might behold unto them where they sit in this time, an it so were that their eyelids were open, he should see them stare as they were mad, and leeringly look as if they saw the devil. Surely it is good they be wary, for truly the fiend is not far. Some set their eyes in their heads as they were sturdy sheep beaten in the head, and as they should die anon. Some hang their heads on one side as if a worm were in their ears. Some pipe when they should speak, as if there were no spirit in their bodies: and this is the proper condition of an hypocrite. Some cry and whine in their throats, so be they greedy and hasty to say that they think: and this is the condition of heretics, and of them that with presumption and with curiosity of wit will always maintain error.

Many unordained and unseemly practices follow on this error, whoso might perceive all. Nevertheless some there be that be so curious that they can refrain them in great part when they come before men. But might these men be seen in place where they be homely, then I trow they should not be hid. And nevertheless yet I trow that whoso would straitly gainsay their opinion, that they should soon see them burst out in some point; and yet them think that all that ever they do, it is for the love of God and for to maintain the truth. Now truly I hope that unless God shew His merciful miracle to make them soon leave off, they shall love God so long on this manner, that they shall go staring mad to the devil. I say not that the devil hath so perfect a servant in this life, that is deceived and infect with all these fantasies that I set here: and nevertheless yet it may be that one, yea, and many one, be infect with them all. But I say that he hath no perfect hypocrite nor heretic in earth that he is not guilty in some that I have said, or peradventure shall say if God vouchsafeth.

For some men are so cumbered in nice curious customs in bodily bearing, that when they shall ought hear, they writhe their heads on one side quaintly, and up with the chin: they gape with their mouths as they should hear with their mouth and not with their ears. Some when they should speak point with their fingers, either on their fingers, or on their own breasts, or on theirs that they speak to. Some can neither sit still, stand still, nor lie still, unless they be either wagging with their feet or else somewhat doing with their hands. Some row with their arms in time of their speaking, as them needed for to swim over a great water. Some be evermore smiling and laughing at every other word that they speak, as they were giggling girls and nice japing jugglers lacking behaviour. Seemly cheer were full fair, with sober and demure bearing of body and mirth in manner.

I say not that all these unseemly practices be great sins in themselves, nor yet all those that do them be great sinners themselves. But I say if that these unseemly and unordained practices be governors of that man that doth them, insomuch that he may not leave them when he will, then I say that they be tokens of pride and curiosity of wit, and of unordained shewing and covetyse of knowing. And specially they be very tokens of unstableness of heart and unrestfulness of mind, and specially of the lacking of the work of this book. And this is the only reason why that I set so many of these deceits here in this writing; for why, that a ghostly worker shall prove his work by them.

Here Beginneth the Four
and Fiftieth Chapter

*How that by virtue of this work a man is governed full wisely,
and made full seemly as well in body as in soul.*

Whoso had this work, it should govern them full seemly, as
well in body as in soul: and make them full favourable
unto each man or woman that looked upon them. Insomuch,
that the worst favoured man or woman that liveth in this life, an
they might come by grace to work in this work, their favour
should suddenly and graciously be changed: that each good man
that them saw, should be fain and joyful to have them in company, and full much they should think that they were pleased in
spirit and holpen by grace unto God in their presence.

And therefore get this gift whoso by grace get may: for whoso
hath it verily, he shall well con govern himself by the virtue
thereof, and all that longeth unto him. He should well give discretion, if need were, of all natures and all dispositions. He
should well con make himself like unto all that with him com-
muned, whether they were accustomed sinners or none,
without sin in himself: in wondering of all that him saw, and in
drawing of others by help of grace to the work of that same
spirit that he worketh in himself.

His cheer and his words should be full of ghostly wisdom, full
of fire, and of fruit spoken in sober soothfastness without any
falsehood, far from any feigning or piping of hypocrites. For
some there be that with all their might, inner and outer, imag-
ineth in their speaking how they may stuff them and underprop

them on each side from falling, with many meek piping words and gestures of devotion: more looking after for to seem holy in sight of men, than for to be so in the sight of God and His angels. For why, these folk will more weigh, and more sorrow make for an unordained gesture or unseemly or unfitting word spoken before men, than they will for a thousand vain thoughts and stinking stirrings of sin wilfully drawn upon them, or recklessly used in the sight of God and the saints and the angels in heaven. Ah, Lord God! where there be any pride within, there such meek piping words be so plenteous without. I grant well, that it is fitting and seemly to them that be meek within, for to shew meek and seemly words and gestures without, according to that meekness that is within in the heart. But I say not that they shall then be shewed in broken nor in piping voices, against the plain disposition of their nature that speak them. For why, if they be true, then be they spoken in soothfastness, and in wholeness of voice and of their spirit that speak them. And if he that hath a plain and an open boisterous voice by nature speak them poorly and pipingly—I mean but if he be sick in his body, or else that it be betwixt him and his God or his confessor—then it is a very token of hypocrisy. I mean either young hypocrisy or old.

And what shall I more say of these venomous deceits? Truly I trow, unless they have grace to leave off such piping hypocrisy, that betwixt that privy pride in their hearts within and such meek words without, the silly soul may full soon sink into sorrow.

Here Beginneth the Five and Fiftieth Chapter

How they be deceived that follow the fervour of spirit in condemning of some without discretion.

Some men the fiend will deceive on this manner. Full wonderfully he will enflame their brains to maintain God's law, and to destroy sin in all other men. He will never tempt them with a thing that is openly evil; he maketh them like busy prelates watching over all the degrees of Christian men's living, as an abbot over his monks. All men will they reprove of their defaults, right as they had cure of their souls: and yet they think that they do not else for God, unless they tell them their defaults that they see. And they say that they be stirred thereto by the fire of charity, and of God's love in their hearts: and truly they lie, for it is with the fire of hell, welling in their brains and in their imagination.

That this is sooth, it seemeth by this that followeth. The devil is a spirit, and of his own nature he hath no body, more than hath an angel. But yet nevertheless what time that he or an angel shall take any body by leave of God, to make any ministration to any man in this life; according as the work is that he shall minister, thereafter in likeness is the quality of his body in some part. Ensample of this we have in Holy Writ. As oft as any angel was sent in body in the Old Testament and in the New also, evermore it was shewed, either by his name or by some instrument or quality of his body, what his matter or his message was in spirit. On the same manner it fareth of the fiend. For

96

when he appeareth in body, he figureth in some quality of his body what his servants be in spirit. Ensample of this may be seen in one instead of all these other. For as I have conceived by some disciples of necromancy, the which have it in science for to make advocation of wicked spirits, and by some unto whom the fiend hath appeared in bodily likeness; that in what bodily likeness the fiend appeareth, evermore he hath but one nostril, and that is great and wide, and he will gladly cast it up that a man may see in thereat to his brain up in his head. The which brain is nought else but the fire of hell, for the fiend may have none other brain; and if he might make a man look in thereto, he wants no better. For at that looking, he should lose his wits for ever. But a perfect prentice of necromancy knoweth this well enough, and can well ordain therefore, so that he provoke him not.

Therefore it is that I say, and have said, that evermore when the devil taketh any body, he figureth in some quality of his body what his servants be in spirit. For he enflameth so the imagination of his contemplatives with the fire of hell, that suddenly without discretion they shoot out their curious conceits, and without any advisement they will take upon them to blame other men's defaults over soon: and this is because they have but one nostril ghostly. For that division that is in a man's nose bodily, and the which departeth the one nostril from the tother, betokeneth that a man should have discretion ghostly; and can dissever the good from the evil, and the evil from the worse, and the good from the better, ere that he gave any full doom of anything that he heard or saw done or spoken about him. And by a man's brain is ghostly understood imagination; for by nature it dwelleth and worketh in the head.

Here Beginneth the Six and Fiftieth Chapter

How they be deceived that lean more to the curiosity of natural wit, and of clergy learned in the school of men, than to the common doctrine and counsel of Holy Church.

Some there be, that although they be not deceived with this error as it is set here, yet for pride and curiosity of natural wit and letterly cunning leave the common doctrine and the counsel of Holy Church. And these with all their favourers lean over much to their own knowing: and for they were never grounded in meek blind feeling and virtuous living, therefore they merit to have a false feeling, feigned and wrought by the ghostly enemy. Insomuch, that at the last they burst up and blaspheme all the saints, sacraments, statutes, and ordinances of Holy Church. Fleshly living men of the world, the which think the statutes of Holy Church over hard to be amended by, they lean to these heretics full soon and full lightly, and stalwartly maintain them, and all because them think that they lead them a softer way than is ordained of Holy Church.

Now truly I trow, that who that will not go the strait way to heaven, that they shall go the soft way to hell. Each man prove by himself, for I trow that all such heretics, and all their favourers, an they might clearly be seen as they shall on the last day, should be seen full soon cumbered in great and horrible sins of the world in their foul flesh, privily, without their open presumption in maintaining of error: so that they be full properly called Antichrist's disciples. For it is said of them, that for all their false fairness openly, yet they should be full foul lechers privily.

Here Beginneth the Seven and Fiftieth Chapter

How these young presumptuous disciples misunderstand this other word "up"; and of the deceits that follow thereon.

No more of these at this time now: but forth of our matter, how that these young presumptuous ghostly disciples misunderstand this other word *up*.

For if it so be, that they either read, or hear read or spoken, how that men should lift up their hearts unto God, as fast they stare in the stars as if they would be above the moon, and hearken when they shall hear any angel sing out of heaven. These men will sometime with the curiosity of their imagination pierce the planets, and make an hole in the firmament to look in thereat. These men will make a God as them list, and clothe Him full richly in clothes, and set Him in a throne far more curiously than ever was He depicted in this earth. These men will make angels in bodily likeness, and set them about each one with diverse minstrelsy, far more curious than ever was any seen or heard in this life. Some of these men the devil will deceive full wonderfully. For he will send a manner of dew, angels' food they ween it be, as it were coming out of the air, and softly and sweetly falling in their mouths; and therefore they have it in custom to sit gaping as they would catch flies. Now truly all this is but deceit, seem it never so holy; for they have in this time full empty souls of any true devotion. Much vanity and falsehood is in their hearts, caused of their curious working. Insomuch, that ofttimes the devil feigneth quaint sounds in their ears, quaint lights and shining in their eyes, and wonderful smells in their noses: and all is but falsehood. And yet ween they not so, for them think that they have ensample of Saint Martin of this upward looking and working, that saw by revelation God clad in his mantle amongst His angels, and of Saint Stephen that saw our Lord stand in heaven, and of many other; and of Christ, that ascended bodily to heaven, seen of His disciples. And therefore they say that we should have our eyes up thither. I grant well that in our bodily observance we should lift up our eyes and our hands if we be stirred in spirit. But I say that the work of our spirit shall not be direct neither upwards nor downwards, nor on one side nor on other, nor forward nor backward, as it is of a bodily thing. For why, our work should be ghostly not bodily, nor on a bodily manner wrought.

Here Beginneth the Eight
and Fiftieth Chapter

That a man shall not take ensample of Saint Martin and of Saint Stephen, for to strain his imagination bodily upwards in the time of his prayer.

For that that they say of Saint Martin and of Saint Stephen, although they saw such things with their bodily eyes, it was shewed but in miracle and in certifying of thing that was ghostly. For wit they right well that Saint Martin's mantle came never on Christ's own body substantially, for no need that He had thereto to keep Him from cold: but by miracle and in likeness for all us that be able to be saved, that be oned to the body of Christ ghostly. And whoso clotheth a poor man and doth any other good deed for God's love bodily or ghostly to any that hath need, sure be they they do it unto Christ ghostly: and they shall be rewarded as substantially therefore as they had done it to Christ's own body. Thus saith Himself in the gospel. And yet thought He it not enough, but if He affirmed it after by miracle; and for this cause He shewed Him unto Saint Martin by revelation. All the revelations that ever saw any man here in bodily likeness in this life, they have ghostly bemeanings. And I trow that if they unto whom they were shewed had been so ghostly, or could have conceived their bemeanings ghostly, that then they had never been shewed bodily. And therefore let us pick off the rough bark, and feed us off the sweet kernel.

But how? Not as these heretics do, the which be well likened to madmen having this custom, that ever when they have drunken of a fair cup, cast it to the wall and break it. Thus should not we do if we will well do. For we should not so feed us of the fruit, that we should despise the tree; nor so drink, that we should break the cup when we have drunken. The tree and the cup I call this visible miracle, and all seemly bodily observances, that is according and not letting the work of the spirit. The fruit and the drink I call the ghostly bemeaning of these visible miracles, and of these seemly bodily observances: as is lifting up of our eyes and our hands unto heaven. If they be done by stirring of the spirit, then be they well done; and else be they hypocrisy, and then be they false. If they be true and contain in them ghostly fruit, why should they then be despised? For men will kiss the cup for wine is therein.

And what thereof, though our Lord when He ascended to heaven bodily took His way upwards into the clouds, seen of His mother and His disciples with their bodily eyes? Should we therefore in our ghostly work ever stare upwards with our bodily eyes, to look after Him if we may see Him sit bodily in heaven, or else stand, as Saint Stephen did? Nay, surely He shewed Him not unto Saint Stephen bodily in heaven, because that He would give us ensample that we should in our ghostly work look bodily up into heaven if we might see Him as Saint Stephen did, either standing, or sitting, or else lying. For howso His body is in heaven—standing, sitting, or lying—wots no man. And it needeth not more to be witted, but that His body is oned with the soul, without departing. The body and the soul, the which is the manhood, is oned with the Godhead without departing also. Of His sitting, His standing, His lying, needeth it not to wit; but that He is there as Him list, and hath Him in body as most seemly is unto Him for to be. For if He shew Him lying, or standing, or sitting, by revelation bodily to any creature in this life, it is done for some ghostly bemeaning: and not for no manner of bodily bearing that He hath in heaven. See by ensample. By standing is understood a readiness of helping. And therefore it is said commonly of one friend to another, when he is in bodily battle: "Bear thee well, fellow, and fight fast, and give not up the battle over lightly; for I shall stand by thee." He meaneth not only bodily standing; for peradventure this battle is on horse and not on foot, and peradventure it is in going and not standing. But he meaneth when he saith that he shall stand by him, that he shall be ready to help him. For this reason it was that our Lord shewed Him bodily in heaven to Saint Stephen, when he was in his martyrdom: and not to give us ensample to look up to heaven. As He had said thus to Saint Stephen in person of all those that suffer persecution for His love: "Lo, Stephen! as verily as I open this bodily firmament, the which is called heaven, and let thee see My bodily standing, trust fast that as verily stand I beside thee ghostly by the might of My Godhead. And I am ready to help thee, and therefore stand thou stiffly in the faith and suffer boldly the fell buffets of those hard stones: for I shall crown thee in bliss for thy meed, and not only thee, but all those that suffer persecution for Me on any manner." And thus mayest thou see that these bodily shewings were done by ghostly bemeanings.

Here Beginneth the Nine and Fiftieth Chapter

That a man shall not take ensample at the bodily ascension of Christ, for to strain his imagination upwards bodily in the time of prayer: and that time, place, and body, these three should be forgotten in all ghostly working.

A nd if thou say aught touching the ascension of our Lord, for that was done bodily, and for a bodily bemeaning as well as for a ghostly, for both He ascended very God and very man: to this will I answer thee, that He had been dead, and was clad with undeadliness, and so shall we be at the Day of Doom. And then we shall be made so subtle in body and in soul together, that we shall be then as swiftly where us list bodily as we be now in our thought ghostly; whether it be up or down, on one side or on other, behind or before, all I hope shall then be alike good, as clerks say. But now thou mayest not come to heaven bodily, but ghostly. And yet it shall be so ghostly, that it shall not be on bodily manner; neither upwards nor downwards, nor on one side nor on other, behind nor before.

And wit well that all those that set them to be ghostly workers, and specially in the work of this book, that although they read "lift up" or "go in," although all that the work of this book be called a stirring, nevertheless yet them behoveth to have a full busy beholding, that this stirring stretch neither up bodily, nor in bodily, nor yet that it be any such stirring as is from one place to another. And although that it be sometime called a rest, nevertheless yet they shall not think that it is any such rest as is any abiding in a place without removing therefrom. For the perfection of this work is so pure and so ghostly in itself, that an it be well and truly conceived, it shall be seen far removed from any stirring and from any place.

And it should by some reason rather be called a sudden changing, than any stirring of place. For time, place, and body: these three should be forgotten in all ghostly working. And therefore be wary in this work, that thou take none ensample at the bodily ascension of Christ for to strain thine imagination in the time of thy prayer bodily upwards, as thou wouldest climb above the moon. For it should on nowise be so, ghostly. But if thou shouldest ascend into heaven bodily, as Christ did, then thou mightest take ensample at it: but that may none do but God, as Himself witnesseth, saying: "There is no man that may ascend unto heaven but only He that descended from heaven, and became man for the love of man." And if it were possible, as it on nowise may be, yet it should be for abundance of ghostly working only by the might of the spirit, full far from any bodily stressing or straining of our imagination bodily, either up, or in, on one side, or on other. And therefore let be such falsehood: it should not be so.

Here Beginneth the Sixtieth Chapter

That the high and the next way to heaven is run by desires, and not by paces of feet.

But now peradventure thou sayest, that how should it then be? For thee thinkest that thou hast very evidence that heaven is upwards; for Christ ascended the air bodily upwards, and sent the Holy Ghost as He promised coming from above bodily, seen of all His disciples; and this is our belief. And therefore thee thinkest since thou hast thus very evidence, why shalt thou not direct thy mind upward bodily in the time of thy prayer?

And to this will I answer thee so feebly as I can, and say: since it so was, that Christ should ascend bodily and thereafter send the Holy Ghost bodily, then it was more seemly that it was upwards and from above than either downwards and from beneath, behind, or before, on one side or on other. But else than for this seemliness, Him needed never the more to have went upwards than downwards; I mean for nearness of the way. For heaven ghostly is as nigh down as up, and up as down: behind as before, before as behind, on one side as other. Insomuch, that whoso had a true desire for to be at heaven, then that same time he were in heaven ghostly. For the high and the next way thither is run by desires, and not by paces of feet. And therefore saith Saint Paul of himself and many other thus; although our bodies be presently here in earth, nevertheless yet our living is in heaven. He meant their love and their desire, the which is ghostly their life. And surely as verily is a soul there where it loveth, as in the body that liveth by it and to the which it giveth life. And therefore if we will go to heaven ghostly, it needeth not to strain our spirit neither up nor down, nor on one side nor on other.

Here Beginneth the One
and Sixtieth Chapter

That all bodily thing is subject unto ghostly thing, and is ruled thereafter by the course of nature and not contrariwise.

Nevertheless it is needful to lift up our eyes and our hands bodily, as it were unto yon bodily heaven, in the which the elements be fastened. I mean if we be stirred of the work of our spirit, and else not. For all bodily thing is subject unto ghostly thing, and is ruled thereafter, and not contrariwise.

Ensample hereof may be seen by the ascension of our Lord: for when the time appointed was come, that Him liked to wend to His Father bodily in His manhood, the which was never nor never may be absent in His Godhead, then mightily by the virtue of the Spirit God, the manhood with the body followed in onehead of person. The visibility of this was most seemly, and most according, to be upward.

This same subjection of the body to the spirit may be in manner verily conceived in the proof of this ghostly work of this book, by them that work therein. For what time that a soul disposeth him effectually to this work, then as fast suddenly, unwitting himself that worketh, the body that peradventure before ere he began was somewhat bent downwards, on one side or on other for ease of the flesh, by virtue of the spirit shall set it upright: following in manner and in likeness bodily the work of the spirit that is made ghostly. And thus it is most seemly to be.

And for this seemliness it is, that a man—the which is the seemliest creature in body that ever God made—is not made crooked to the earthwards, as be an other beasts, but upright to heavenwards. For why? That it should figure in likeness bodily the work of the soul ghostly; the which falleth to be upright ghostly, and not crooked ghostly. Take heed that I say upright ghostly, and not bodily. For how should a soul, the which in his nature hath no manner thing of bodilyness, be strained upright bodily? Nay, it may not be.

And therefore be wary that thou conceive not bodily that which is meant ghostly, although it be spoken in bodily words, as be these, up or down, in or out, behind or before, on one side or on other. For although that a thing be never so ghostly in itself, nevertheless yet if it shall be spoken of, since it so is that speech is a bodily work wrought with the tongue, the which is an instrument of the body, it behoveth always be spoken in bodily words. But what thereof? Shall it therefore be taken and conceived bodily? Nay, but ghostly, as it be meant.

Here Beginneth the Two and Sixtieth Chapter

How a man may wit when his ghostly work is beneath him or without him, and when it is even with him or within him, and when it is above him and under his God.

And for this, that thou shalt be able better to wit how they shall be conceived ghostly, these words that be spoken bodily, therefore I think to declare to thee the ghostly bemeaning of some words that fall to ghostly working. So that thou mayest wit clearly without error when thy ghostly work is beneath thee and without thee, and when it is within thee and even with thee, and when it is above thee and under thy God.

All manner of bodily thing is without thy soul and beneath it in nature, yea! the sun and the moon and all the stars, although they be above thy body, nevertheless yet they be beneath thy soul.

All angels and all souls, although they be confirmed and adorned with grace and with virtues, for the which they be above thee in cleanness, nevertheless, yet they be but even with thee in nature.

Within in thyself in nature be the powers of thy soul: the which be these three principal, Memory, Reason, and Will; and secondary, Imagination and Sensuality.

Above thyself in nature is no manner of thing but only God.

Evermore where thou findest written thyself in ghostliness, then it is understood thy soul, and not thy body. And then all after that thing is on the which the powers of thy soul work, thereafter shall the worthiness and the condition of thy work be deemed; whether it be beneath thee, within thee, or above thee.

Here Beginneth the Three and Sixtieth Chapter

Of the powers of a soul in general, and how Memory in special is a principal power, comprehending in it all the other powers and all those things in the which they work.

Memory is such a power in itself, that properly to speak and in manner, it worketh not itself. But Reason and Will, they be two working powers, and so is Imagination and Sensuality also. And all these four powers and their works, Memory containeth and comprehendeth in itself. And otherwise it is not said that the Memory worketh, unless such a comprehension be a work.

And therefore it is that I call the powers of a soul, some principal, and some secondary. Not because a soul is divisible, for that may not be: but because all those things in the which they work be divisible, and some principal, as be all ghostly things, and some secondary, as be all bodily things. The two principal working powers, Reason and Will, work purely in themselves in all ghostly things, without help of the other two secondary powers. Imagination and Sensuality work beastly in all bodily things, whether they be present or absent, in the body and with the bodily wits. But by them, without help of Reason and of Will, may a soul never come to for to know the virtue and the conditions of bodily creatures, nor the cause of their beings and their makings.

And for this cause is Reason and Will called principal powers, for they work in pure spirit without any manner of bodilyness: and Imagination and Sensuality secondary, for they work in the body with bodily instruments, the which be our five wits. Memory is called a principal power, for it containeth in it ghostly not only all the other powers, but thereto all those things in the which they work. See by the proof.

Here Beginneth the Four
and Sixtieth Chapter

Of the other two principal powers, Reason and Will; and of the work of them before sin and after.

Reason is a power through the which we depart the evil from the good, the evil from the worse, the good from the better, the worse from the worst, the better from the best. Before ere man sinned, might Reason have done all this by nature. But now it is so blinded with the original sin, that it may not con work this work, unless it be illumined by grace. And both the self Reason, and the thing that it worketh in, be comprehended and contained in the Memory.

Will is a power through the which we choose good, after that it be determined with Reason; and through the which we love good, we desire good, and rest us with full liking and consent endlessly in God. Before ere man sinned, might not Will be deceived in his choosing, in his loving, nor in none of his works. For why, it had then by nature to savour each thing as it was; but now it may not do so, unless it be anointed with grace. For ofttimes because of infection of the original sin, it savoureth a thing for good that is full evil, and that hath but the likeness of good. And both the Will and the thing that is willed, the Memory containeth and comprehendeth in it.

Here Beginneth the Five and Sixtieth Chapter

Of the first secondary power, Imagination by name; and of the works and the obedience of it unto Reason, before sin and after.

Imagination is a power through the which we portray all images of absent and present things, and both it and the thing that it worketh in be contained in the Memory. Before ere man sinned, was Imagination so obedient unto the Reason, to the which it is as it were servant, that it ministered never to it any unordained image of any bodily creature, or any fantasy of any ghostly creature: but now it is not so. For unless it be refrained by the light of grace in the Reason, else it will never cease, sleeping or waking, for to portray diverse unordained images of bodily creatures; or else some fantasy, the which is nought else but a bodily conceit of a ghostly thing, or else a ghostly conceit of a bodily thing. And this is evermore feigned and false, and next unto error.

This inobedience of the Imagination may clearly be conceived in them that be newlings turned from the world unto devotion, in the time of their prayer. For before the time be, that the Imagination be in great part refrained by the light of grace in the Reason, as it is in continual meditation of ghostly things—as be their own wretchedness, the passion and the kindness of our Lord God, with many such other—they may in nowise put away the wonderful and the diverse thoughts, fantasies, and images, the which be ministered and printed in their mind by the light of the curiosity of Imagination. And all this inobedience is the pain of the original sin.

Here Beginneth the Six and Sixtieth Chapter

Of the other secondary power, Sensuality by name; and of the works and of the obedience of it unto Will, before sin and after.

Sensuality is a power of our soul, recking and reigning in the bodily wits, through the which we have bodily knowing and feeling of all bodily creatures, whether they be pleasing or unpleasing. And it hath two parts: one through the which it beholdeth to the needfulness of our body, another through the which it serveth to the lusts of the bodily wits. For this same power is it, that grumbleth when the body lacketh the needful things unto it, and that in the taking of the need stirreth us to take more than needeth in feeding and furthering of our lusts: that grumbleth in lacking of pleasing creatures, and lustily is delighted in their presence: that grumbleth in presence of mis-liking creatures, and is lustily pleased in their absence. Both this power and the thing that it worketh in be contained in the Memory.

Before ere man sinned was the Sensuality so obedient unto the Will, unto the which it is as it were servant, that it ministered never unto it any unordained liking or grumbling in any bodily creature, or any ghostly feigning of liking or misliking made by any ghostly enemy in the bodily wits. But now it is not so: for unless it be ruled by grace in the Will, for to suffer meekly and in measure the pain of the original sin, the which it feeleth in absence of needful comforts and in presence of speedful dis-comforts, and thereto also for to restrain it from lust in presence of needful comforts, and from lusty plesaunce in the absence of speedful discomforts: else will it wretchedly and wantonly wel-ter, as a swine in the mire, in the wealths of this world and the foul flesh so much that all our living shall be more beastly and fleshly, than either manly or ghostly.

Here Beginneth the Seven and Sixtieth Chapter

That whoso knoweth not the powers of a soul and the manner of her working, may lightly be deceived in understanding of ghostly words and of ghostly working; and how a soul is made a God in Grace.

L o, ghostly friend! to such wretchedness as thou here mayest see be we fallen for sin: and therefore what wonder is it, though we be blindly and lightly deceived in understanding of ghostly words and of ghostly working, and specially those the which know not yet the powers of their souls and the manners of their working?

For ever when the Memory is occupied with any bodily thing, be it taken to never so good an end, yet thou art beneath thyself in this working, and without any soul. And ever when thou feelest thy Memory occupied with the subtle conditions of the powers of thy soul and their workings in ghostly things, as be vices or virtues, of thyself, or of any creature that is ghostly and even with thee in nature, to that end that thou mightest by this work learn to know thyself in furthering of perfection: then thou art within thyself, and even with thyself. But ever when thou feelest thy Memory occupied with no manner of thing that is bodily or ghostly, but only with the self substance of God, as it is and may be, in the proof of the work of this book: then thou art above thyself and beneath thy God.

Above thyself thou art: for why, thou attainest to come thither by grace, whither thou mayest not come by nature. That is to say, to be oned to God, in spirit, and in love, and in accordance of will. Beneath thy God thou art: for why, although it may be said in manner, that in this time God and thou be not two but one in spirit—insomuch that thou or another, for such onehead that feeleth the perfection of this work, may soothfastly by witness of Scripture be called a God—nevertheless yet thou art beneath Him. For why, He is God by nature without beginning; and thou, that sometime wert nought in substance, and thereto after when thou wert by His might and His love made ought, wilfully with sin madest thyself worse than nought, only by His mercy without thy desert are made a God in grace, oned with Him in spirit without departing, both here and in bliss of heaven without any end. So that, although thou be all one with Him in grace, yet thou art full far beneath Him in nature.

Lo, ghostly friend! hereby mayest thou see somewhat in part, that whoso knoweth not the powers of their own soul, and the manner of their working, may full lightly be deceived in understanding of words that be written to ghostly intent. And therefore mayest thou see somewhat the cause why that I durst not plainly bid thee shew thy desire unto God, but I bade thee childishly do that in thee is to hide it and cover it. And this I do for fear lest thou shouldest conceive bodily that that is meant ghostly.

Here Beginneth the Eight and Sixtieth Chapter

That nowhere bodily, is everywhere ghostly; and how our outer man calleth the work of this book nought.

A nd on the same manner, where another man would bid thee gather thy powers and thy wits wholly within thyself, and worship God there—although he say full well and full truly, yea! and no man trulier, an he be well conceived—yet for fear of deceit and bodily conceiving of his words, me list not bid thee do so. But thus will I bid thee. Look on nowise that thou be within thyself. And shortly, without thyself will I not that thou be, nor yet above, nor behind, nor on one side, nor on other.

"Where then," sayest thou, "shall I be? Nowhere, by thy tale!" Now truly thou sayest well; for there would I have thee. For why, nowhere bodily, is everywhere ghostly. Look then busily that thy ghostly work be nowhere bodily; and then wheresoever that that thing is, on the which thou wilfully workest in thy mind in substance, surely there art thou in spirit, as verily as thy body is in that place that thou art bodily. And although thy bodily wits can find there nothing to feed them on, for them think it nought that thou dost, yea! do on then this nought, and do it for God's love. And let not therefore, but travail busily in that nought with a waking desire to will to have God that no man may know. For I tell thee truly, that I had rather be so nowhere bodily, wrestling with that blind nought, than to be so great a lord that I might when I would be everywhere bodily, merrily playing with all this ought as a lord with his own.

Let be this everywhere and this ought, in comparison of this nowhere and this nought. Reck thee never if thy wits cannot reason of this nought; for surely, I love it much the better. It is so worthy a thing in itself, that they cannot reason thereupon. This nought may better be felt than seen: for it is full blind and full dark to them that have but little while looked thereupon. Nevertheless, if I shall soothlier say, a soul is more blinded in feeling of it for abundance of ghostly light, than for any darkness or wanting of bodily light. What is he that calleth it nought? Surely it is our outer man, and not our inner. Our inner man calleth it All; for of it he is well learned to know the reason of all things bodily or ghostly, without any special beholding to any one thing by itself.

Here Beginneth the Nine
and Sixtieth Chapter

How that a man's affection is marvellously changed in ghostly feeling of this nought, when it is nowhere wrought.

Wonderfully is a man's affection varied in ghostly feeling of this nought when it is nowhere wrought. For at the first time that a soul looketh thereupon, it shall find all the special deeds of sin that ever he did since he was born, bodily or ghostly, privily or darkly painted thereupon. And howsoever that he turneth it about, evermore they will appear before his eyes; until the time be, that with much hard travail, many sore sighings, and many bitter weepings, he have in great part washed them away. Sometime in this travail him think that it is to look thereupon as on hell; for him think that he despaireth to win to perfection of ghostly rest out of that pain. Thus far inwards come many, but for greatness of pain that they feel and for lacking of comfort, they go back in beholding of bodily things: seeking fleshly comforts without, for lacking of ghostly they have not yet deserved, as they should if they had abided.

For he that abideth feeleth sometime some comfort, and hath some hope of perfection; for he feeleth and seeth that many of his fordone special sins be in great part by help of grace rubbed away. Nevertheless yet ever among he feeleth pain, but he thinketh that it shall have an end, for it waxeth ever less and less. And therefore he calleth it nought else but purgatory. Sometime he can find no special sin written thereupon, but yet him think that sin is a lump, he wot never what, none other thing than

118

himself; and then it may be called the base and the pain of the original sin. Sometime him think that it is paradise or heaven, for diverse wonderful sweetness and comforts, joys and blessed virtues that he findeth therein. Sometime him think it God, for peace and rest that he findeth therein.

Yea! think what he think will; for evermore he shall find it *a cloud of unknowing*, that is betwixt him and his God.

Here Beginneth
the Seventieth Chapter

That right as by the defailing of our bodily wits we begin more readily to come to knowing of ghostly things, so by the defailing of our ghostly wits we begin most readily to come to the knowledge of God, such as is possible by grace to be had here.

And therefore travail fast in this nought, and this nowhere, and leave thine outward bodily wits and all that they work in: for I tell thee truly, that this work may not be conceived by them.

For by thine eyes thou mayest not conceive of anything, unless it be by the length and the breadth, the smallness and the greatness, the roundness and the squareness, the farness and the nearness, and the colour of it. And by thine ears, nought but noise or some manner of sound. By thine nose, nought but either stench or savour. And by thy taste, nought but either sour or sweet, salt or fresh, bitter or liking. And by thy feeling, nought but either hot or cold, hard or tender, soft or sharp. And truly, neither hath God nor ghostly things none of these qualities nor quantities. And therefore leave thine outward wits, and work not with them, neither within nor without: for all those that set them to be ghostly workers within, and ween that they should either hear, smell, or see, taste or feel, ghostly things, either within them or without, surely they be deceived, and work wrong against the course of nature.

For by nature they be ordained, that with them men should have knowing of all outward bodily things, and on nowise by them come to the knowing of ghostly things. I mean by their works. By their failings we may, as thus: when we read or hear speak of some certain things, and thereto conceive that our outward wits cannot tell us by no quality what those things be, then we may be verily certified that those things be ghostly things, and not bodily things.

On this same manner ghostly it fareth within our ghostly wits, when we travail about the knowing of God Himself. For have a man never so much ghostly understanding in knowing of all made ghostly things, yet may he never by the work of his understanding come to the knowing of an unmade ghostly thing: the which is nought but God. But by the failing it may: for why, that thing that it faileth in is nothing else but only God. And therefore it was that Saint Denis said, *the most goodly knowing of God is that, the which is known by unknowing.* And truly, whoso will look in Denis' books, he shall find that his words will clearly affirm all that I have said or shall say, from the beginning of this treatise to the end. On otherwise than thus, list me not cite him, nor none other doctor, for me at this time. For sometime, men thought it meekness to say nought of their own heads, unless they affirmed it by Scripture and doctors' words: and now it is turned into curiosity, and shewing of cunning. To thee it needeth not, and therefore I do it not. For whoso hath ears, let him hear, and whoso is stirred for to trow, let him trow: for else, shall they not.

Here Beginneth the One
and Seventieth Chapter

That some may not come to feel the perfection of this work but in time of ravishing, and some may have it when they will, in the common state of man's soul.

Some think this matter so hard and so fearful, that they say it may not be come to without much strong travail coming before, nor conceived but seldom, and that but in the time of ravishing. And to these men will I answer as feebly as I can, and say, that it is all at the ordinance and the disposition of God, after their ableness in soul that this grace of contemplation and of ghostly working is given to.

For some there be that without much and long ghostly exercise may not come thereto, and yet it shall be but full seldom, and in special calling of our Lord that they shall feel the perfection of this work: the which calling is called ravishing. And some there be that be so subtle in grace and in spirit, and so homely with God in this grace of contemplation, that they may have it when they will in the common state of man's soul: as it is in sitting, going, standing, or kneeling. And yet in this time they have full deliberation of all their wits bodily or ghostly, and may use them if they desire: not without some letting (but without great letting). Ensample of the first we have by Moses, and of this other by Aaron the priest of the Temple: for why, this grace of contemplation is figured by the Ark of the Testament in the old law, and the workers in this grace be figured by them that most meddled them about this Ark, as the story will witness. And well is this grace and this work likened unto that Ark. For right as in that Ark were contained all the jewels and the relics of the Temple, right so in this little love put upon this cloud be contained all the virtues of man's soul, the which is the ghostly Temple of God.

Moses ere he might come to see this Ark and for to wit how it should be made, with great long travail he clomb up to the top of the mountain, and dwelled there, and wrought in a cloud six days: abiding unto the seventh day that our Lord would vouchsafe for to shew unto him the manner of this Ark-making. By Moses's long travail and his late shewing, be understood those that may not come to the perfection of this ghostly work without long travail coming before: and yet but full seldom, and when God will vouchsafe to shew it.

But that that Moses might not come to see but seldom, and that not without great long travail, Aaron had in his power because of his office, for to see it in the Temple within the Veil as oft as him liked for to enter. And by this Aaron is understood all those the which I spake of above, the which by their ghostly cunning, by help of grace, may assign unto them the perfection of this work as them liketh.

Here Beginneth the Two and Seventieth Chapter

That a worker in this work should not deem nor think of another worker as he feeleth in himself.

L o! hereby mayest thou see that he that may not come for to see and feel the perfection of this work but by long travail, and yet is it but seldom, may lightly be deceived if he speak, think, and deem other men as he feeleth in himself, that they may not come to it but seldom, and that not without great travail. And on the same manner may he be deceived that may have it when he will, if he deem all other thereafter; saying that they may have it when they will. Let be this: nay, surely he may not think thus. For peradventure, when it liketh unto God, that those that may not at the first time have it but seldom, and that not without great travail, sithen after they shall have it when they will, as oft as them liketh. Ensample of this we have of Moses, that first but seldom, and not without great travail, in the mount might not see the manner of the Ark: and sithen after, as oft as by him liked, saw it in the Veil.

Here Beginneth the Three
and Seventieth Chapter

*How that after the likeness of Moses, of Bezaleel, and of Aaron
meddling them about the Ark of the Testament, we profit on
three manners in this grace of contemplation, for this grace is
figured in that Ark.*

Three men there were that most principally meddled them
with this Ark of the Old Testament: Moses, Bezaleel, Aaron.
Moses learned in the mount of our Lord how it should be made.
Bezaleel wrought it and made it in the Veil after the ensample
that was shewed in the mountain. And Aaron had it in keeping
in the Temple, to feel it and see it as oft as him liked.

At the likeness of these three, we profit on three manners in
this grace of contemplation. Sometime we profit only by grace,
and then we be likened unto Moses, that for all the climbing and
the travail that he had into the mount might not come to see it
but seldom: and yet was that sight only by the shewing of our
Lord when Him liked to shew it, and not for any desert of his
travail. Sometime we profit in this grace by our own ghostly cunning, helped with grace, and then be we likened to Bezaleel, the
which might not see the Ark ere the time that he had made it by
his own travail, helped with the ensample that was shewed unto
Moses in the mount. And sometime we profit in this grace by
other men's teaching, and then be we likened to Aaron, the
which had it in keeping and in custom to see and feel the Ark
when him pleased, that Bezaleel had wrought and made ready
before to his hands.

Lo! ghostly friend, in this work, though it be childishly and lewdly spoken, I bear, though I be a wretch unworthy to teach any creature, the office of Bezaleel: making and declaring in manner to thine hands the manner of this ghostly Ark. But far better and more worthily than I do, thou mayest work if thou wilt be Aaron: that is to say, continually working therein for thee and for me. Do then so I pray thee, for the love of God Almighty. And since we be both called of God to work in this work, I beseech thee for God's love fulfil in thy part what lacketh of mine.

Here Beginneth the Four
and Seventieth Chapter

How that the matter of this book is never more read or spoken, nor heard read or spoken, of a soul disposed thereto without feeling of a very accordance to the effect of the same work: and of rehearsing of the same charge that is written in the prologue.

And if thee think that this manner of working be not according to thy disposition in body and in soul, thou mayest leave it and take another, safely with good ghostly counsel without blame. And then I beseech thee that thou wilt have me excused, for truly I would have profited unto thee in this writing at my simple cunning; and that was mine intent. And therefore read over twice or thrice; and ever the ofter the better, and the more thou shalt conceive thereof. Insomuch, peradventure, that some sentence that was full hard to thee at the first or the second reading, soon after thou shalt think it easy.

Yea! and it seemeth impossible to mine understanding, that any soul that is disposed to this work should read it or speak it, or else hear it read or spoken, but if that same soul should feel for that time a very accordance to the effect of this work. And then if thee think it doth thee good, thank God heartily, and for God's love pray for me.

Do then so. And I pray thee for God's love that thou let none see this book, unless it be such one that thee think is like to the book; after that thou findest written in the book before, where it telleth what men and when they should work in this work. And if thou shalt let any such men see it, then I pray thee that thou bid them take them time to look it all over. For peradventure there is some matter therein in the beginning, or in the midst, the which is hanging and not fully declared there as it standeth. But if it be not there, it is soon after, or else in the end. And thus if a man saw one part and not another, peradventure he should lightly be led into error: and therefore I pray thee to work as I say thee. And if thee think that there be any matter therein that thou wouldest have more opened than it is, let me wit which it is, and thy conceit thereupon; and at my simple cunning it shall be amended if I can.

Fleshly janglers, flatterers and blamers, ronkers and ronners, and all manner of pinchers, cared I never that they saw this book: for mine intent was never to write such thing to them. And therefore I would not that they heard it, neither they nor none of these curious lettered nor unlearned men: yea! although they be full good men in active living, for it accordeth not to them.

Here Beginneth the Five
and Seventieth Chapter

Of some certain tokens by the which a man may prove whether
he be called of God to work in this work.

A ll those that read or hear the matter of this book be read or
spoken, and in this reading or hearing think it a good and
liking thing, be never the rather called of God to work in this
work, only for this liking stirring that they feel in the time of
this reading. For peradventure this stirring cometh more of a
natural curiosity of wit, than of any calling of grace.

But if they will prove whence this stirring cometh, they may
prove thus, if them liketh. First let them look if they have done
that in them is before, abling them thereto in cleansing of their
conscience at the doom of Holy Church, their counsel according.
If it be thus, it is well inasmuch: but if they will wit more near, let
them look if it be evermore pressing in their remembrance more
customably than is any other of ghostly exercise. And if them
think that there is no manner of thing that they do, bodily or
ghostly, that is sufficiently done with witness of their conscience,
unless this privy little love pressed be in manner ghostly the chief
of all their work: and if they thus feel, then it is a token that they
be called of God to this work, and surely else not.

I say not that it shall ever last and dwell in all their minds continually, that be called to work in this work. Nay, so is it not. For
from a young ghostly prentice in this work, the actual feeling
thereof is ofttimes withdrawn for divers reasons. Sometime, for
he shall not take over presumptuously thereupon, and ween that

it be in great part in his own power to have it when him list, and as him list. And such a weening were pride. And evermore when the feeling of grace is withdrawn, pride is the cause: not ever pride that is, but pride that should be, were it not that this feeling of grace were withdrawn. And thus ween ofttimes some young fools, that God is their enemy; when He is their full friend.

Sometimes it is withdrawn for their carelessness; and when it is thus, they feel soon after a full bitter pain that beateth them full sore. Sometimes our Lord will delay it by an artful device, for He will by such a delaying make it grow, and be had more in dainty when it is new found and felt again that long had been lost. And this is one of the readiest and sovereignest tokens that a soul may have to wit by, whether he be called or not to work in this work, if he feel after such a delaying and a long lacking of this work, that when it cometh suddenly as it doth, unpurchased with any means, that he hath then a greater fervour of desire and greater love longing to work in this work, than ever he had any before. Insomuch, that ofttimes I trow, he hath more joy of the finding thereof than ever he had sorrow of the losing.

And if it be thus, surely it is a very token without error, that he is called of God to work in this work, whatsoever that he be or hath been.

For not what thou art, nor what thou hast been, beholdeth God with His merciful eyes; but that thou wouldest be. And Saint Gregory to witness, that all holy desires grow by delays: and if they wane by delays, then were they never holy desires. For he that feeleth ever less joy and less, in new findings and sudden presentations of his old purposed desires, although they may be called natural desires to the good, nevertheless holy desires were they never. Of this holy desire speaketh Saint Austin and saith, that all the life of a good Christian man is nought else but holy desire.

Farewell, ghostly friend, in God's blessing and mine! And I beseech Almighty God, that true peace, holy counsel, and ghostly comfort in God with abundance of grace, evermore be with thee and all God's lovers in earth. Amen.

HERE ENDETH THE CLOUD OF UNKNOWING.

A CATALOG OF SELECTED
DOVER BOOKS
IN ALL FIELDS OF INTEREST

A CATALOG OF SELECTED DOVER
BOOKS IN ALL FIELDS OF INTEREST

CONCERNING THE SPIRITUAL IN ART, Wassily Kandinsky. Pioneering work by father of abstract art. Thoughts on color theory, nature of art. Analysis of earlier masters. 12 illustrations. 80pp. of text. 5⅜ x 8½.   23411-8

ANIMALS: 1,419 Copyright-Free Illustrations of Mammals, Birds, Fish, Insects, etc., Jim Harter (ed.). Clear wood engravings present, in extremely lifelike poses, over 1,000 species of animals. One of the most extensive pictorial sourcebooks of its kind. Captions. Index. 284pp. 9 x 12.   23766-4

CELTIC ART: The Methods of Construction, George Bain. Simple geometric techniques for making Celtic interlacements, spirals, Kells-type initials, animals, humans, etc. Over 500 illustrations. 160pp. 9 x 12. (Available in U.S. only.)   22923-8

AN ATLAS OF ANATOMY FOR ARTISTS, Fritz Schider. Most thorough reference work on art anatomy in the world. Hundreds of illustrations, including selections from works by Vesalius, Leonardo, Goya, Ingres, Michelangelo, others. 593 illustrations. 192pp. 7⅛ x 10¼.   20241-0

CELTIC HAND STROKE-BY-STROKE (Irish Half-Uncial from "The Book of Kells"): An Arthur Baker Calligraphy Manual, Arthur Baker. Complete guide to creating each letter of the alphabet in distinctive Celtic manner. Covers hand position, strokes, pens, inks, paper, more. Illustrated. 48pp. 8¼ x 11.   24336-2

EASY ORIGAMI, John Montroll. Charming collection of 32 projects (hat, cup, pelican, piano, swan, many more) specially designed for the novice origami hobbyist. Clearly illustrated easy-to-follow instructions insure that even beginning papercrafters will achieve successful results. 48pp. 8¼ x 11.   27298-2

THE COMPLETE BOOK OF BIRDHOUSE CONSTRUCTION FOR WOOD-WORKERS, Scott D. Campbell. Detailed instructions, illustrations, tables. Also data on bird habitat and instinct patterns. Bibliography. 3 tables. 63 illustrations in 15 figures. 48pp. 5¼ x 8½.   24407-5

BLOOMINGDALE'S ILLUSTRATED 1886 CATALOG: Fashions, Dry Goods and Housewares, Bloomingdale Brothers. Famed merchants' extremely rare catalog depicting about 1,700 products: clothing, housewares, firearms, dry goods, jewelry, more. Invaluable for dating, identifying vintage items. Also, copyright-free graphics for artists, designers. Co-published with Henry Ford Museum & Greenfield Village. 160pp. 8¼ x 11.   25780-0

HISTORIC COSTUME IN PICTURES, Braun & Schneider. Over 1,450 costumed figures in clearly detailed engravings–from dawn of civilization to end of 19th century. Captions. Many folk costumes. 256pp. 8⅜ x 11¾.   23150-X

CATALOG OF DOVER BOOKS

STICKLEY CRAFTSMAN FURNITURE CATALOGS, Gustav Stickley and L. &
J. G. Stickley. Beautiful, functional furniture in two authentic catalogs from 1910. 594
illustrations, including 277 photos, show settles, rockers, armchairs, reclining chairs,
bookcases, desks, tables. 183pp. 6½ x 9¼.   23838-5

AMERICAN LOCOMOTIVES IN HISTORIC PHOTOGRAPHS: 1858 to 1949,
Ron Ziel (ed.). A rare collection of 126 meticulously detailed official photographs,
called "builder portraits," of American locomotives that majestically chronicle the
rise of steam locomotive power in America. Introduction. Detailed captions. xi+
129pp. 9 x 12.   27393-8

AMERICA'S LIGHTHOUSES: An Illustrated History, Francis Ross Holland, Jr.
Delightfully written, profusely illustrated fact-filled survey of over 200 American lighthouses since 1716. History, anecdotes, technological advances, more. 240pp. 8 x 10¾.
                                                                             25576-X

TOWARDS A NEW ARCHITECTURE, Le Corbusier. Pioneering manifesto by
founder of "International School." Technical and aesthetic theories, views of industry, eco-
nomics, relation of form to function, "mass-production split" and much more. Profusely
illustrated. 320pp. 6⅛ x 9¼. (Available in U.S. only.)   25023-7

HOW THE OTHER HALF LIVES, Jacob Riis. Famous journalistic record, expos-
ing poverty and degradation of New York slums around 1900, by major social
reformer. 100 striking and influential photographs. 233pp. 10 x 7⅞.   22012-5

FRUIT KEY AND TWIG KEY TO TREES AND SHRUBS, William M. Harlow.
One of the handiest and most widely used identification aids. Fruit key covers 120
deciduous and evergreen species; twig key 160 deciduous species. Easily used. Over
300 photographs. 126pp. 5⅜ x 8½.   20511-8

COMMON BIRD SONGS, Dr. Donald J. Borror. Songs of 60 most common U.S.
birds: robins, sparrows, cardinals, bluejays, finches, more–arranged in order of
increasing complexity. Up to 9 variations of songs of each species.
                                                  Cassette and manual 99911-4

ORCHIDS AS HOUSE PLANTS, Rebecca Tyson Northen. Grow cattleyas and
many other kinds of orchids–in a window, in a case, or under artificial light. 63 illustrations. 148pp. 5⅜ x 8½.   23261-1

MONSTER MAZES, Dave Phillips. Masterful mazes at four levels of difficulty.
Avoid deadly perils and evil creatures to find magical treasures. Solutions for all 32
exciting illustrated puzzles. 48pp. 8¼ x 11.   26005-4

MOZART'S DON GIOVANNI (DOVER OPERA LIBRETTO SERIES),
Wolfgang Amadeus Mozart. Introduced and translated by Ellen H. Bleiler. Standard
Italian libretto, with complete English translation. Convenient and thoroughly
portable–an ideal companion for reading along with a recording or the performance
itself. Introduction. List of characters. Plot summary. 121pp. 5¼ x 8½.   24944-1

TECHNICAL MANUAL AND DICTIONARY OF CLASSICAL BALLET, Gail
Grant. Defines, explains, comments on steps, movements, poses and concepts. 15-
page pictorial section. Basic book for student, viewer. 127pp. 5⅜ x 8½.   21843-0

CATALOG OF DOVER BOOKS

THE CLARINET AND CLARINET PLAYING, David Pino. Lively, comprehensive work features suggestions about technique, musicianship, and musical interpretation, as well as guidelines for teaching, making your own reeds, and preparing for public performance. Includes an intriguing look at clarinet history. "A godsend," *The Clarinet,* Journal of the International Clarinet Society. Appendixes. 7 illus. 320pp. 5⅜ x 8½. 40270-3

HOLLYWOOD GLAMOR PORTRAITS, John Kobal (ed.). 145 photos from 1926-49. Harlow, Gable, Bogart, Bacall; 94 stars in all. Full background on photographers, technical aspects. 160pp. 8⅜ x 11¼. 23352-9

THE ANNOTATED CASEY AT THE BAT: A Collection of Ballads about the Mighty Casey/Third, Revised Edition, Martin Gardner (ed.). Amusing sequels and parodies of one of America's best-loved poems: Casey's Revenge, Why Casey Whiffed, Casey's Sister at the Bat, others. 256pp. 5⅜ x 8½. 28598-7

THE RAVEN AND OTHER FAVORITE POEMS, Edgar Allan Poe. Over 40 of the author's most memorable poems: "The Bells," "Ulalume," "Israfel," "To Helen," "The Conqueror Worm," "Eldorado," "Annabel Lee," many more. Alphabetic lists of titles and first lines. 64pp. 5 3⁄16 x 8¼. 26685-0

PERSONAL MEMOIRS OF U. S. GRANT, Ulysses Simpson Grant. Intelligent, deeply moving firsthand account of Civil War campaigns, considered by many the finest military memoirs ever written. Includes letters, historic photographs, maps and more. 528pp. 6⅛ x 9¼. 28587-1

ANCIENT EGYPTIAN MATERIALS AND INDUSTRIES, A. Lucas and J. Harris. Fascinating, comprehensive, thoroughly documented text describes this ancient civilization's vast resources and the processes that incorporated them in daily life, including the use of animal products, building materials, cosmetics, perfumes and incense, fibers, glazed ware, glass and its manufacture, materials used in the mummification process, and much more. 544pp. 6⅛ x 9¼. (Available in U.S. only.) 40446-3

RUSSIAN STORIES/RUSSKIE RASSKAZY: A Dual-Language Book, edited by Gleb Struve. Twelve tales by such masters as Chekhov, Tolstoy, Dostoevsky, Pushkin, others. Excellent word-for-word English translations on facing pages, plus teaching and study aids, Russian/English vocabulary, biographical/critical introductions, more. 416pp. 5⅜ x 8½. 26244-8

PHILADELPHIA THEN AND NOW: 60 Sites Photographed in the Past and Present, Kenneth Finkel and Susan Oyama. Rare photographs of City Hall, Logan Square, Independence Hall, Betsy Ross House, other landmarks juxtaposed with contemporary views. Captures changing face of historic city. Introduction. Captions. 128pp. 8¼ x 11. 25790-8

AIA ARCHITECTURAL GUIDE TO NASSAU AND SUFFOLK COUNTIES, LONG ISLAND, The American Institute of Architects, Long Island Chapter, and the Society for the Preservation of Long Island Antiquities. Comprehensive, well-researched and generously illustrated volume brings to life over three centuries of Long Island's great architectural heritage. More than 240 photographs with authoritative, extensively detailed captions. 176pp. 8¼ x 11. 26946-9

NORTH AMERICAN INDIAN LIFE: Customs and Traditions of 23 Tribes, Elsie Clews Parsons (ed.). 27 fictionalized essays by noted anthropologists examine religion, customs, government, additional facets of life among the Winnebago, Crow, Zuni, Eskimo, other tribes. 480pp. 6⅛ x 9¼. 27377-6

FRANK LLOYD WRIGHT'S DANA HOUSE, Donald Hoffmann. Pictorial essay of residential masterpiece with over 160 interior and exterior photos, plans, elevations, sketches and studies. 128pp. 9¼ x 10¾. 29120-0

THE MALE AND FEMALE FIGURE IN MOTION: 60 Classic Photographic Sequences, Eadweard Muybridge. 60 true-action photographs of men and women walking, running, climbing, bending, turning, etc., reproduced from rare 19th-century masterpiece. vi + 121pp. 9 x 12. 24745-7

1001 QUESTIONS ANSWERED ABOUT THE SEASHORE, N. J. Berrill and Jacquelyn Berrill. Queries answered about dolphins, sea snails, sponges, starfish, fishes, shore birds, many others. Covers appearance, breeding, growth, feeding, much more. 305pp. 5¼ x 8¼. 23366-9

ATTRACTING BIRDS TO YOUR YARD, William J. Weber. Easy-to-follow guide offers advice on how to attract the greatest diversity of birds: birdhouses, feeders, water and waterers, much more. 96pp. 5³⁄₁₆ x 8¼. 28927-3

MEDICINAL AND OTHER USES OF NORTH AMERICAN PLANTS: A Historical Survey with Special Reference to the Eastern Indian Tribes, Charlotte Erichsen-Brown. Chronological historical citations document 500 years of usage of plants, trees, shrubs native to eastern Canada, northeastern U.S. Also complete identifying information. 343 illustrations. 544pp. 6½ x 9¼. 25951-X

STORYBOOK MAZES, Dave Phillips. 23 stories and mazes on two-page spreads: Wizard of Oz, Treasure Island, Robin Hood, etc. Solutions. 64pp. 8¼ x 11. 23628-5

AMERICAN NEGRO SONGS: 230 Folk Songs and Spirituals, Religious and Secular, John W. Work. This authoritative study traces the African influences of songs sung and played by black Americans at work, in church, and as entertainment. The author discusses the lyric significance of such songs as "Swing Low, Sweet Chariot," "John Henry," and others and offers the words and music for 230 songs. Bibliography. Index of Song Titles. 272pp. 6½ x 9¼. 40271-1

MOVIE-STAR PORTRAITS OF THE FORTIES, John Kobal (ed.). 163 glamor, studio photos of 106 stars of the 1940s: Rita Hayworth, Ava Gardner, Marlon Brando, Clark Gable, many more. 176pp. 8⅜ x 11¼. 23546-7

BENCHLEY LOST AND FOUND, Robert Benchley. Finest humor from early 30s, about pet peeves, child psychologists, post office and others. Mostly unavailable elsewhere. 73 illustrations by Peter Arno and others. 183pp. 5⅜ x 8½. 22410-4

YEKL and THE IMPORTED BRIDEGROOM AND OTHER STORIES OF YIDDISH NEW YORK, Abraham Cahan. Film Hester Street based on *Yekl* (1896). Novel, other stories among first about Jewish immigrants on N.Y.'s East Side. 240pp. 5⅜ x 8½. 22427-9

SELECTED POEMS, Walt Whitman. Generous sampling from *Leaves of Grass*. Twenty-four poems include "I Hear America Singing," "Song of the Open Road," "I Sing the Body Electric," "When Lilacs Last in the Dooryard Bloom'd," "O Captain! My Captain!"–all reprinted from an authoritative edition. Lists of titles and first lines. 128pp. 5³⁄₁₆ x 8¼. 26878-0

THE BEST TALES OF HOFFMANN, E. T. A. Hoffmann. 10 of Hoffmann's most important stories: "Nutcracker and the King of Mice," "The Golden Flowerpot," etc. 458pp. 5⅜ x 8½. 21793-0

FROM FETISH TO GOD IN ANCIENT EGYPT, E. A. Wallis Budge. Rich detailed survey of Egyptian conception of "God" and gods, magic, cult of animals, Osiris, more. Also, superb English translations of hymns and legends. 240 illustrations. 545pp. 5⅜ x 8½. 25803-3

FRENCH STORIES/CONTES FRANÇAIS: A Dual-Language Book, Wallace Fowlie. Ten stories by French masters, Voltaire to Camus: "Micromegas" by Voltaire; "The Atheist's Mass" by Balzac; "Minuet" by de Maupassant; "The Guest" by Camus, six more. Excellent English translations on facing pages. Also French-English vocabulary list, exercises, more. 352pp. 5⅜ x 8½. 26443-2

CHICAGO AT THE TURN OF THE CENTURY IN PHOTOGRAPHS: 122 Historic Views from the Collections of the Chicago Historical Society, Larry A. Viskochil. Rare large-format prints offer detailed views of City Hall, State Street, the Loop, Hull House, Union Station, many other landmarks, circa 1904-1913. Introduction. Captions. Maps. 144pp. 9⅜ x 12¼. 24656-6

OLD BROOKLYN IN EARLY PHOTOGRAPHS, 1865-1929, William Lee Younger. Luna Park, Gravesend race track, construction of Grand Army Plaza, moving of Hotel Brighton, etc. 157 previously unpublished photographs. 165pp. 8⅞ x 11¾. 23587-4

THE MYTHS OF THE NORTH AMERICAN INDIANS, Lewis Spence. Rich anthology of the myths and legends of the Algonquins, Iroquois, Pawnees and Sioux, prefaced by an extensive historical and ethnological commentary. 36 illustrations. 480pp. 5⅜ x 8½. 25967-6

AN ENCYCLOPEDIA OF BATTLES: Accounts of Over 1,560 Battles from 1479 B.C. to the Present, David Eggenberger. Essential details of every major battle in recorded history from the first battle of Megiddo in 1479 B.C. to Grenada in 1984. List of Battle Maps. New Appendix covering the years 1967-1984. Index. 99 illustrations. 544pp. 6½ x 9¼. 24913-1

SAILING ALONE AROUND THE WORLD, Captain Joshua Slocum. First man to sail around the world, alone, in small boat. One of great feats of seamanship told in delightful manner. 67 illustrations. 294pp. 5⅜ x 8½. 20326-3

ANARCHISM AND OTHER ESSAYS, Emma Goldman. Powerful, penetrating, prophetic essays on direct action, role of minorities, prison reform, puritan hypocrisy, violence, etc. 271pp. 5⅜ x 8½. 22484-8

MYTHS OF THE HINDUS AND BUDDHISTS, Ananda K. Coomaraswamy and Sister Nivedita. Great stories of the epics; deeds of Krishna, Shiva, taken from puranas, Vedas, folk tales; etc. 32 illustrations. 400pp. 5⅜ x 8½. 21759-0

THE TRAUMA OF BIRTH, Otto Rank. Rank's controversial thesis that anxiety neurosis is caused by profound psychological trauma which occurs at birth. 256pp. 5⅜ x 8½. 27974-X

A THEOLOGICO-POLITICAL TREATISE, Benedict Spinoza. Also contains unfinished Political Treatise. Great classic on religious liberty, theory of government on common consent. R. Elwes translation. Total of 421pp. 5⅜ x 8½. 20249-6

CATALOG OF DOVER BOOKS

MY BONDAGE AND MY FREEDOM, Frederick Douglass. Born a slave, Douglass became outspoken force in antislavery movement. The best of Douglass' autobiographies. Graphic description of slave life. 464pp. 5⅜ x 8½. 22457-0

FOLLOWING THE EQUATOR: A Journey Around the World, Mark Twain. Fascinating humorous account of 1897 voyage to Hawaii, Australia, India, New Zealand, etc. Ironic, bemused reports on peoples, customs, climate, flora and fauna, politics, much more. 197 illustrations. 720pp. 5⅜ x 8½. 26113-1

THE PEOPLE CALLED SHAKERS, Edward D. Andrews. Definitive study of Shakers: origins, beliefs, practices, dances, social organization, furniture and crafts, etc. 33 illustrations. 351pp. 5⅜ x 8½. 21081-2

THE MYTHS OF GREECE AND ROME, H. A. Guerber. A classic of mythology, generously illustrated, long prized for its simple, graphic, accurate retelling of the principal myths of Greece and Rome, and for its commentary on their origins and significance. With 64 illustrations by Michelangelo, Raphael, Titian, Rubens, Canova, Bernini and others. 480pp. 5⅜ x 8½. 27584-1

PSYCHOLOGY OF MUSIC, Carl E. Seashore. Classic work discusses music as a medium from psychological viewpoint. Clear treatment of physical acoustics, auditory apparatus, sound perception, development of musical skills, nature of musical feeling, host of other topics. 88 figures. 408pp. 5⅜ x 8½. 21851-1

THE PHILOSOPHY OF HISTORY, Georg W. Hegel. Great classic of Western thought develops concept that history is not chance but rational process, the evolution of freedom. 457pp. 5⅜ x 8½. 20112-0

THE BOOK OF TEA, Kakuzo Okakura. Minor classic of the Orient: entertaining, charming explanation, interpretation of traditional Japanese culture in terms of tea ceremony. 94pp. 5⅜ x 8½. 20070-1

LIFE IN ANCIENT EGYPT, Adolf Erman. Fullest, most thorough, detailed older account with much not in more recent books, domestic life, religion, magic, medicine, commerce, much more. Many illustrations reproduce tomb paintings, carvings, hieroglyphs, etc. 597pp. 5⅜ x 8½. 22632-8

SUNDIALS, Their Theory and Construction, Albert Waugh. Far and away the best, most thorough coverage of ideas, mathematics concerned, types, construction, adjusting anywhere. Simple, nontechnical treatment allows even children to build several of these dials. Over 100 illustrations. 230pp. 5⅜ x 8½. 22947-5

THEORETICAL HYDRODYNAMICS, L. M. Milne-Thomson. Classic exposition of the mathematical theory of fluid motion, applicable to both hydrodynamics and aerodynamics. Over 600 exercises. 768pp. 6⅛ x 9¼. 68970-0

SONGS OF EXPERIENCE: Facsimile Reproduction with 26 Plates in Full Color, William Blake. 26 full-color plates from a rare 1826 edition. Includes "The Tyger," "London," "Holy Thursday," and other poems. Printed text of poems. 48pp. 5¼ x 7. 24636-1

OLD-TIME VIGNETTES IN FULL COLOR, Carol Belanger Grafton (ed.). Over 390 charming, often sentimental illustrations, selected from archives of Victorian graphics—pretty women posing, children playing, food, flowers, kittens and puppies, smiling cherubs, birds and butterflies, much more. All copyright-free. 48pp. 9¼ x 12¼. 27269-9

PERSPECTIVE FOR ARTISTS, Rex Vicat Cole. Depth, perspective of sky and sea, shadows, much more, not usually covered. 391 diagrams, 81 reproductions of drawings and paintings. 279pp. 5⅜ x 8½. 22487-2

DRAWING THE LIVING FIGURE, Joseph Sheppard. Innovative approach to artistic anatomy focuses on specifics of surface anatomy, rather than muscles and bones. Over 170 drawings of live models in front, back and side views, and in widely varying poses. Accompanying diagrams. 177 illustrations. Introduction. Index. 144pp. 8⅜ x11¼. 26723-7

GOTHIC AND OLD ENGLISH ALPHABETS: 100 Complete Fonts, Dan X. Solo. Add power, elegance to posters, signs, other graphics with 100 stunning copyright-free alphabets: Blackstone, Dolbey, Germania, 97 more–including many lower-case, numerals, punctuation marks. 104pp. 8⅛ x 11. 24695-7

HOW TO DO BEADWORK, Mary White. Fundamental book on craft from simple projects to five-bead chains and woven works. 106 illustrations. 142pp. 5⅜ x 8. 20697-1

THE BOOK OF WOOD CARVING, Charles Marshall Sayers. Finest book for beginners discusses fundamentals and offers 34 designs. "Absolutely first rate . . . well thought out and well executed."–E. J. Tangerman. 118pp. 7¾ x 10⅝. 23654-4

ILLUSTRATED CATALOG OF CIVIL WAR MILITARY GOODS: Union Army Weapons, Insignia, Uniform Accessories, and Other Equipment, Schuyler, Hartley, and Graham. Rare, profusely illustrated 1846 catalog includes Union Army uniform and dress regulations, arms and ammunition, coats, insignia, flags, swords, rifles, etc. 226 illustrations. 160pp. 9 x 12. 24939-5

WOMEN'S FASHIONS OF THE EARLY 1900s: An Unabridged Republication of "New York Fashions, 1909," National Cloak & Suit Co. Rare catalog of mail-order fashions documents women's and children's clothing styles shortly after the turn of the century. Captions offer full descriptions, prices. Invaluable resource for fashion, costume historians. Approximately 725 illustrations. 128pp. 8⅜ x 11¼. 27276-1

THE 1912 AND 1915 GUSTAV STICKLEY FURNITURE CATALOGS, Gustav Stickley. With over 200 detailed illustrations and descriptions, these two catalogs are essential reading and reference materials and identification guides for Stickley furniture. Captions cite materials, dimensions and prices. 112pp. 6½ x 9¼. 26676-1

EARLY AMERICAN LOCOMOTIVES, John H. White, Jr. Finest locomotive engravings from early 19th century: historical (1804–74), main-line (after 1870), special, foreign, etc. 147 plates. 142pp. 11⅜ x 8¼. 22772-3

THE TALL SHIPS OF TODAY IN PHOTOGRAPHS, Frank O. Braynard. Lavishly illustrated tribute to nearly 100 majestic contemporary sailing vessels: Amerigo Vespucci, Clearwater, Constitution, Eagle, Mayflower, Sea Cloud, Victory, many more. Authoritative captions provide statistics, background on each ship. 190 black-and-white photographs and illustrations. Introduction. 128pp. 8⅞ x 11¾. 27163-3

LITTLE BOOK OF EARLY AMERICAN CRAFTS AND TRADES, Peter Stockham (ed.). 1807 children's book explains crafts and trades: baker, hatter, cooper, potter, and many others. 23 copperplate illustrations. 140pp. 4⅝ x 6.   23336-7

VICTORIAN FASHIONS AND COSTUMES FROM HARPER'S BAZAR, 1867–1898, Stella Blum (ed.). Day costumes, evening wear, sports clothes, shoes, hats, other accessories in over 1,000 detailed engravings. 320pp. 9⅜ x 12¼. 22990-4

GUSTAV STICKLEY, THE CRAFTSMAN, Mary Ann Smith. Superb study surveys broad scope of Stickley's achievement, especially in architecture. Design philosophy, rise and fall of the Craftsman empire, descriptions and floor plans for many Craftsman houses, more. 86 black-and-white halftones. 31 line illustrations. Introduction 208pp. 6½ x 9¼.   27210-9

THE LONG ISLAND RAIL ROAD IN EARLY PHOTOGRAPHS, Ron Ziel. Over 220 rare photos, informative text document origin (1844) and development of rail service on Long Island. Vintage views of early trains, locomotives, stations, passengers, crews, much more. Captions. 8⅞ x 11¾.   26301-0

VOYAGE OF THE LIBERDADE, Joshua Slocum. Great 19th-century mariner's thrilling, first-hand account of the wreck of his ship off South America, the 35-foot boat he built from the wreckage, and its remarkable voyage home. 128pp. 5⅜ x 8½.
40022-0

TEN BOOKS ON ARCHITECTURE, Vitruvius. The most important book ever written on architecture. Early Roman aesthetics, technology, classical orders, site selection, all other aspects. Morgan translation. 331pp. 5⅜ x 8½.   20645-9

THE HUMAN FIGURE IN MOTION, Eadweard Muybridge. More than 4,500 stopped-action photos, in action series, showing undraped men, women, children jumping, lying down, throwing, sitting, wrestling, carrying, etc. 390pp. 7⅞ x 10⅝.
20204-6 Clothbd.

TREES OF THE EASTERN AND CENTRAL UNITED STATES AND CANADA, William M. Harlow. Best one-volume guide to 140 trees. Full descriptions, woodlore, range, etc. Over 600 illustrations. Handy size. 288pp. 4½ x 6⅜.   20395-6

SONGS OF WESTERN BIRDS, Dr. Donald J. Borror. Complete song and call repertoire of 60 western species, including flycatchers, juncoes, cactus wrens, many more–includes fully illustrated booklet.   Cassette and manual 99913-0

GROWING AND USING HERBS AND SPICES, Milo Miloradovich. Versatile handbook provides all the information needed for cultivation and use of all the herbs and spices available in North America. 4 illustrations. Index. Glossary. 236pp. 5⅜ x 8½.
25058-X

BIG BOOK OF MAZES AND LABYRINTHS, Walter Shepherd. 50 mazes and labyrinths in all–classical, solid, ripple, and more–in one great volume. Perfect inexpensive puzzler for clever youngsters. Full solutions. 112pp. 8⅛ x 11.   22951-3

PIANO TUNING, J. Cree Fischer. Clearest, best book for beginner, amateur. Simple repairs, raising dropped notes, tuning by easy method of flattened fifths. No previous skills needed. 4 illustrations. 201pp. 5⅜ x 8½. 23267-0

HINTS TO SINGERS, Lillian Nordica. Selecting the right teacher, developing confidence, overcoming stage fright, and many other important skills receive thoughtful discussion in this indispensible guide, written by a world-famous diva of four decades' experience. 96pp. 5⅜ x 8½. 40094-8

THE COMPLETE NONSENSE OF EDWARD LEAR, Edward Lear. All nonsense limericks, zany alphabets, Owl and Pussycat, songs, nonsense botany, etc., illustrated by Lear. Total of 320pp. 5⅜ x 8½. (Available in U.S. only.) 20167-8

VICTORIAN PARLOUR POETRY: An Annotated Anthology, Michael R. Turner. 117 gems by Longfellow, Tennyson, Browning, many lesser-known poets. "The Village Blacksmith," "Curfew Must Not Ring Tonight," "Only a Baby Small," dozens more, often difficult to find elsewhere. Index of poets, titles, first lines. xxiii + 325pp. 5⅜ x 8¼. 27044-0

DUBLINERS, James Joyce. Fifteen stories offer vivid, tightly focused observations of the lives of Dublin's poorer classes. At least one, "The Dead," is considered a masterpiece. Reprinted complete and unabridged from standard edition. 160pp. 5³⁄₁₆ x 8¼. 26870-5

GREAT WEIRD TALES: 14 Stories by Lovecraft, Blackwood, Machen and Others, S. T. Joshi (ed.). 14 spellbinding tales, including "The Sin Eater," by Fiona McLeod, "The Eye Above the Mantel," by Frank Belknap Long, as well as renowned works by R. H. Barlow, Lord Dunsany, Arthur Machen, W. C. Morrow and eight other masters of the genre. 256pp. 5⅜ x 8½. (Available in U.S. only.) 40436-6

THE BOOK OF THE SACRED MAGIC OF ABRAMELIN THE MAGE, translated by S. MacGregor Mathers. Medieval manuscript of ceremonial magic. Basic document in Aleister Crowley, Golden Dawn groups. 268pp. 5⅜ x 8½. 23211-5

NEW RUSSIAN-ENGLISH AND ENGLISH-RUSSIAN DICTIONARY, M. A. O'Brien. This is a remarkably handy Russian dictionary, containing a surprising amount of information, including over 70,000 entries. 366pp. 4½ x 6⅛. 20208-9

HISTORIC HOMES OF THE AMERICAN PRESIDENTS, Second, Revised Edition, Irvin Haas. A traveler's guide to American Presidential homes, most open to the public, depicting and describing homes occupied by every American President from George Washington to George Bush. With visiting hours, admission charges, travel routes. 175 photographs. Index. 160pp. 8¼ x 11. 26751-2

NEW YORK IN THE FORTIES, Andreas Feininger. 162 brilliant photographs by the well-known photographer, formerly with *Life* magazine. Commuters, shoppers, Times Square at night, much else from city at its peak. Captions by John von Hartz. 181pp. 9¼ x 10¾. 23585-8

INDIAN SIGN LANGUAGE, William Tomkins. Over 525 signs developed by Sioux and other tribes. Written instructions and diagrams. Also 290 pictographs. 111pp. 6⅛ x 9¼. 22029-X

CATALOG OF DOVER BOOKS

ANATOMY: A Complete Guide for Artists, Joseph Sheppard. A master of figure drawing shows artists how to render human anatomy convincingly. Over 460 illustrations. 224pp. 8⅜ x 11¼. 27279-6

MEDIEVAL CALLIGRAPHY: Its History and Technique, Marc Drogin. Spirited history, comprehensive instruction manual covers 13 styles (ca. 4th century through 15th). Excellent photographs; directions for duplicating medieval techniques with modern tools. 224pp. 8⅜ x 11¼. 26142-5

DRIED FLOWERS: How to Prepare Them, Sarah Whitlock and Martha Rankin. Complete instructions on how to use silica gel, meal and borax, perlite aggregate, sand and borax, glycerine and water to create attractive permanent flower arrangements. 12 illustrations. 32pp. 5⅜ x 8½. 21802-3

EASY-TO-MAKE BIRD FEEDERS FOR WOODWORKERS, Scott D. Campbell. Detailed, simple-to-use guide for designing, constructing, caring for and using feeders. Text, illustrations for 12 classic and contemporary designs. 96pp. 5⅜ x 8½.
25847-5

SCOTTISH WONDER TALES FROM MYTH AND LEGEND, Donald A. Mackenzie. 16 lively tales tell of giants rumbling down mountainsides, of a magic wand that turns stone pillars into warriors, of gods and goddesses, evil hags, powerful forces and more. 240pp. 5⅜ x 8½. 29677-6

THE HISTORY OF UNDERCLOTHES, C. Willett Cunnington and Phyllis Cunnington. Fascinating, well-documented survey covering six centuries of English undergarments, enhanced with over 100 illustrations: 12th-century laced-up bodice, footed long drawers (1795), 19th-century bustles, 19th-century corsets for men, Victorian "bust improvers," much more. 272pp. 5⅜ x 8¼. 27124-2

ARTS AND CRAFTS FURNITURE: The Complete Brooks Catalog of 1912, Brooks Manufacturing Co. Photos and detailed descriptions of more than 150 now very collectible furniture designs from the Arts and Crafts movement depict davenports, settees, buffets, desks, tables, chairs, bedsteads, dressers and more, all built of solid, quarter-sawed oak. Invaluable for students and enthusiasts of antiques, Americana and the decorative arts. 80pp. 6½ x 9¼. 27471-3

WILBUR AND ORVILLE: A Biography of the Wright Brothers, Fred Howard. Definitive, crisply written study tells the full story of the brothers' lives and work. A vividly written biography, unparalleled in scope and color, that also captures the spirit of an extraordinary era. 560pp. 6⅛ x 9¼. 40297-5

THE ARTS OF THE SAILOR: Knotting, Splicing and Ropework, Hervey Garrett Smith. Indispensable shipboard reference covers tools, basic knots and useful hitches; handsewing and canvas work, more. Over 100 illustrations. Delightful reading for sea lovers. 256pp. 5⅜ x 8½. 26440-8

FRANK LLOYD WRIGHT'S FALLINGWATER: The House and Its History, Second, Revised Edition, Donald Hoffmann. A total revision—both in text and illustrations—of the standard document on Fallingwater, the boldest, most personal architectural statement of Wright's mature years, updated with valuable new material from the recently opened Frank Lloyd Wright Archives. "Fascinating"—*The New York Times*. 116 illustrations. 128pp. 9¼ x 10¾. 27430-6

CATALOG OF DOVER BOOKS

PHOTOGRAPHIC SKETCHBOOK OF THE CIVIL WAR, Alexander Gardner. 100 photos taken on field during the Civil War. Famous shots of Manassas Harper's Ferry, Lincoln, Richmond, slave pens, etc. 244pp. 10⅝ x 8¼.   22731-6

FIVE ACRES AND INDEPENDENCE, Maurice G. Kains. Great back-to-the-land classic explains basics of self-sufficient farming. The one book to get. 95 illustrations. 397pp. 5⅜ x 8½.   20974-1

SONGS OF EASTERN BIRDS, Dr. Donald J. Borror. Songs and calls of 60 species most common to eastern U.S.: warblers, woodpeckers, flycatchers, thrushes, larks, many more in high-quality recording.   Cassette and manual 99912-2

A MODERN HERBAL, Margaret Grieve. Much the fullest, most exact, most useful compilation of herbal material. Gigantic alphabetical encyclopedia, from aconite to zedoary, gives botanical information, medical properties, folklore, economic uses, much else. Indispensable to serious reader. 161 illustrations. 888pp. 6½ x 9¼. 2-vol. set. (Available in U.S. only.)   Vol. I: 22798-7
Vol. II: 22799-5

HIDDEN TREASURE MAZE BOOK, Dave Phillips. Solve 34 challenging mazes accompanied by heroic tales of adventure. Evil dragons, people-eating plants, blood-thirsty giants, many more dangerous adversaries lurk at every twist and turn. 34 mazes, stories, solutions. 48pp. 8¼ x 11.   24566-7

LETTERS OF W. A. MOZART, Wolfgang A. Mozart. Remarkable letters show bawdy wit, humor, imagination, musical insights, contemporary musical world; includes some letters from Leopold Mozart. 276pp. 5⅜ x 8½.   22859-2

BASIC PRINCIPLES OF CLASSICAL BALLET, Agrippina Vaganova. Great Russian theoretician, teacher explains methods for teaching classical ballet. 118 illustrations. 175pp. 5⅜ x 8½.   22036-2

THE JUMPING FROG, Mark Twain. Revenge edition. The original story of The Celebrated Jumping Frog of Calaveras County, a hapless French translation, and Twain's hilarious "retranslation" from the French. 12 illustrations. 66pp. 5⅜ x 8½.   22686-7

BEST REMEMBERED POEMS, Martin Gardner (ed.). The 126 poems in this superb collection of 19th- and 20th-century British and American verse range from Shelley's "To a Skylark" to the impassioned "Renascence" of Edna St. Vincent Millay and to Edward Lear's whimsical "The Owl and the Pussycat." 224pp. 5⅜ x 8½.   27165-X

COMPLETE SONNETS, William Shakespeare. Over 150 exquisite poems deal with love, friendship, the tyranny of time, beauty's evanescence, death and other themes in language of remarkable power, precision and beauty. Glossary of archaic terms. 80pp. 5³⁄₁₆ x 8¼.   26686-9

THE BATTLES THAT CHANGED HISTORY, Fletcher Pratt. Eminent historian profiles 16 crucial conflicts, ancient to modern, that changed the course of civilization. 352pp. 5⅜ x 8½.   41129-X

CATALOG OF DOVER BOOKS

THE WIT AND HUMOR OF OSCAR WILDE, Alvin Redman (ed.). More than 1,000 ripostes, paradoxes, wisecracks: Work is the curse of the drinking classes; I can resist everything except temptation; etc. 258pp. 5⅜ x 8½. 20602-5

SHAKESPEARE LEXICON AND QUOTATION DICTIONARY, Alexander Schmidt. Full definitions, locations, shades of meaning in every word in plays and poems. More than 50,000 exact quotations. 1,485pp. 6½ x 9¼. 2-vol. set.
Vol. 1: 22726-X
Vol. 2: 22727-8

SELECTED POEMS, Emily Dickinson. Over 100 best-known, best-loved poems by one of America's foremost poets, reprinted from authoritative early editions. No comparable edition at this price. Index of first lines. 64pp. 5³⁄₁₆ x 8¼. 26466-1

THE INSIDIOUS DR. FU-MANCHU, Sax Rohmer. The first of the popular mystery series introduces a pair of English detectives to their archnemesis, the diabolical Dr. Fu-Manchu. Flavorful atmosphere, fast-paced action, and colorful characters enliven this classic of the genre. 208pp. 5³⁄₁₆ x 8¼. 29898-1

THE MALLEUS MALEFICARUM OF KRAMER AND SPRENGER, translated by Montague Summers. Full text of most important witchhunter's "bible," used by both Catholics and Protestants. 278pp. 6⅝ x 10. 22802-9

SPANISH STORIES/CUENTOS ESPAÑOLES: A Dual-Language Book, Angel Flores (ed.). Unique format offers 13 great stories in Spanish by Cervantes, Borges, others. Faithful English translations on facing pages. 352pp. 5⅜ x 8½. 25399-6

GARDEN CITY, LONG ISLAND, IN EARLY PHOTOGRAPHS, 1869–1919, Mildred H. Smith. Handsome treasury of 118 vintage pictures, accompanied by carefully researched captions, document the Garden City Hotel fire (1899), the Vanderbilt Cup Race (1908), the first airmail flight departing from the Nassau Boulevard Aerodrome (1911), and much more. 96pp. 8⅞ x 11¾. 40669-5

OLD QUEENS, N.Y., IN EARLY PHOTOGRAPHS, Vincent F. Seyfried and William Asadorian. Over 160 rare photographs of Maspeth, Jamaica, Jackson Heights, and other areas. Vintage views of DeWitt Clinton mansion, 1939 World's Fair and more. Captions. 192pp. 8⅞ x 11. 26358-4

CAPTURED BY THE INDIANS: 15 Firsthand Accounts, 1750-1870, Frederick Drimmer. Astounding true historical accounts of grisly torture, bloody conflicts, relentless pursuits, miraculous escapes and more, by people who lived to tell the tale. 384pp. 5⅜ x 8½. 24901-8

THE WORLD'S GREAT SPEECHES (Fourth Enlarged Edition), Lewis Copeland, Lawrence W. Lamm, and Stephen J. McKenna. Nearly 300 speeches provide public speakers with a wealth of updated quotes and inspiration–from Pericles' funeral oration and William Jennings Bryan's "Cross of Gold Speech" to Malcolm X's powerful words on the Black Revolution and Earl of Spenser's tribute to his sister, Diana, Princess of Wales. 944pp. 5⅜ x 8⅜. 40903-1

THE BOOK OF THE SWORD, Sir Richard F. Burton. Great Victorian scholar/adventurer's eloquent, erudite history of the "queen of weapons"–from prehistory to early Roman Empire. Evolution and development of early swords, variations (sabre, broadsword, cutlass, scimitar, etc.), much more. 336pp. 6⅛ x 9¼. 25434-8

AUTOBIOGRAPHY: The Story of My Experiments with Truth, Mohandas K. Gandhi. Boyhood, legal studies, purification, the growth of the Satyagraha (nonviolent protest) movement. Critical, inspiring work of the man responsible for the freedom of India. 480pp. 5⅜ x 8½. (Available in U.S. only.) 24593-4

CELTIC MYTHS AND LEGENDS, T. W. Rolleston. Masterful retelling of Irish and Welsh stories and tales. Cuchulain, King Arthur, Deirdre, the Grail, many more. First paperback edition. 58 full-page illustrations. 512pp. 5⅜ x 8½. 26507-2

THE PRINCIPLES OF PSYCHOLOGY, William James. Famous long course complete, unabridged. Stream of thought, time perception, memory, experimental methods; great work decades ahead of its time. 94 figures. 1,391pp. 5⅜ x 8½. 2-vol. set.
Vol. I: 20381-6 Vol. II: 20382-4

THE WORLD AS WILL AND REPRESENTATION, Arthur Schopenhauer. Definitive English translation of Schopenhauer's life work, correcting more than 1,000 errors, omissions in earlier translations. Translated by E. F. J. Payne. Total of 1,269pp. 5⅜ x 8½. 2-vol. set. Vol. 1: 21761-2 Vol. 2: 21762-0

MAGIC AND MYSTERY IN TIBET, Madame Alexandra David-Neel. Experiences among lamas, magicians, sages, sorcerers, Bonpa wizards. A true psychic discovery. 32 illustrations. 321pp. 5⅜ x 8½. (Available in U.S. only.) 22682-4

THE EGYPTIAN BOOK OF THE DEAD, E. A. Wallis Budge. Complete reproduction of Ani's papyrus, finest ever found. Full hieroglyphic text, interlinear transliteration, word-for-word translation, smooth translation. 533pp. 6½ x 9¼. 21866-X

MATHEMATICS FOR THE NONMATHEMATICIAN, Morris Kline. Detailed, college-level treatment of mathematics in cultural and historical context, with numerous exercises. Recommended Reading Lists. Tables. Numerous figures. 641pp. 5⅜ x 8½.
24823-2

PROBABILISTIC METHODS IN THE THEORY OF STRUCTURES, Isaac Elishakoff. Well-written introduction covers the elements of the theory of probability from two or more random variables, the reliability of such multivariable structures, the theory of random function, Monte Carlo methods of treating problems incapable of exact solution, and more. Examples. 502pp. 5⅜ x 8½. 40691-1

THE RIME OF THE ANCIENT MARINER, Gustave Doré, S. T. Coleridge. Doré's finest work; 34 plates capture moods, subtleties of poem. Flawless full-size reproductions printed on facing pages with authoritative text of poem. "Beautiful. Simply beautiful."–*Publisher's Weekly*. 77pp. 9¼ x 12. 22305-1

NORTH AMERICAN INDIAN DESIGNS FOR ARTISTS AND CRAFTSPEOPLE, Eva Wilson. Over 360 authentic copyright-free designs adapted from Navajo blankets, Hopi pottery, Sioux buffalo hides, more. Geometrics, symbolic figures, plant and animal motifs, etc. 128pp. 8⅜ x 11. (Not for sale in the United Kingdom.) 25341-4

SCULPTURE: Principles and Practice, Louis Slobodkin. Step-by-step approach to clay, plaster, metals, stone; classical and modern. 253 drawings, photos. 255pp. 8⅛ x 11.
22960-2

THE INFLUENCE OF SEA POWER UPON HISTORY, 1660–1783, A. T. Mahan. Influential classic of naval history and tactics still used as text in war colleges. First paperback edition. 4 maps. 24 battle plans. 640pp. 5⅜ x 8½. 25509-3

CATALOG OF DOVER BOOKS

THE STORY OF THE TITANIC AS TOLD BY ITS SURVIVORS, Jack Winocour (ed.). What it was really like. Panic, despair, shocking inefficiency, and a little heroism. More thrilling than any fictional account. 26 illustrations. 320pp. 5⅜ x 8½.
20610-6

FAIRY AND FOLK TALES OF THE IRISH PEASANTRY, William Butler Yeats (ed.). Treasury of 64 tales from the twilight world of Celtic myth and legend: "The Soul Cages," "The Kildare Pooka," "King O'Toole and his Goose," many more. Introduction and Notes by W. B. Yeats. 352pp. 5⅜ x 8½.
26941-8

BUDDHIST MAHAYANA TEXTS, E. B. Cowell and others (eds.). Superb, accurate translations of basic documents in Mahayana Buddhism, highly important in history of religions. The Buddha-karita of Asvaghosha, Larger Sukhavativyuha, more. 448pp. 5⅜ x 8½.
25552-2

ONE TWO THREE . . . INFINITY: Facts and Speculations of Science, George Gamow. Great physicist's fascinating, readable overview of contemporary science: number theory, relativity, fourth dimension, entropy, genes, atomic structure, much more. 128 illustrations. Index. 352pp. 5⅜ x 8½.
25664-2

EXPERIMENTATION AND MEASUREMENT, W. J. Youden. Introductory manual explains laws of measurement in simple terms and offers tips for achieving accuracy and minimizing errors. Mathematics of measurement, use of instruments, experimenting with machines. 1994 edition. Foreword. Preface. Introduction. Epilogue. Selected Readings. Glossary. Index. Tables and figures. 128pp. 5⅜ x 8½.
40451-X

DALÍ ON MODERN ART: The Cuckolds of Antiquated Modern Art, Salvador Dalí. Influential painter skewers modern art and its practitioners. Outrageous evaluations of Picasso, Cézanne, Turner, more. 15 renderings of paintings discussed. 44 calligraphic decorations by Dalí. 96pp. 5⅜ x 8½. (Available in U.S. only.)
29220-7

ANTIQUE PLAYING CARDS: A Pictorial History, Henry René D'Allemagne. Over 900 elaborate, decorative images from rare playing cards (14th–20th centuries): Bacchus, death, dancing dogs, hunting scenes, royal coats of arms, players cheating, much more. 96pp. 9¼ x 12¼.
29265-7

MAKING FURNITURE MASTERPIECES: 30 Projects with Measured Drawings, Franklin H. Gottshall. Step-by-step instructions, illustrations for constructing handsome, useful pieces, among them a Sheraton desk, Chippendale chair, Spanish desk, Queen Anne table and a William and Mary dressing mirror. 224pp. 8⅛ x 11¼.
29338-6

THE FOSSIL BOOK: A Record of Prehistoric Life, Patricia V. Rich et al. Profusely illustrated definitive guide covers everything from single-celled organisms and dinosaurs to birds and mammals and the interplay between climate and man. Over 1,500 illustrations. 760pp. 7½ x 10⅛.
29371-8